Personal Survival Kits

and how to use them effectively

By

David E Crossley

© Copyright 2015   David E Crossley

ISBN-13: 978-1522727378

ISBN-10: 152272737X

All rights reserved. Other than short excerpts for review purposes, or for personal, non-commercial use by the purchaser, no part of this publication may be reproduced, or transmitted, in any form or by any means, electronic, mechanical, photocopying, recording, or otherwise, without the written prior permission of the author.

Cover picture by David E Crossley
Left side: The Friendly Swede Multi-purpose 10-in-1 Survival Kit Paracord Bracelet with Silva watchstrap compass added
Right side: Homemade paracord pouch kit with The Friendly Swede carabiner and Acme Howler whistle

Index

Introduction	5
Choices, choices!	7
Cutting Tools	27
Saws	45
Cordage	55
Fire starters	59
Water	71
Food	75
Navigation	81
Signalling	87
Light sources	94
First aid and medicine	99
Other	103
Basic kit lists	108
Summary	110
Acknowledgements	111
About the author	112

Introduction

One question almost invariably asked by people who are new to the concept of disaster survival, and in particular to Personal Survival Kits (PSKs) is, 'But could you really survive using just what's in that little tin?'

The correct answer to that is, 'No!' You don't survive using just what is in the tin; you survive using the knowledge and skills that you have developed through training and practise. The contents of the tin make that a little easier by providing some tools that prevent you having to start from scratch, at caveman level. Most importantly those tools replace familiar things that either would not be available or would be difficult and stressful to improvise in an emergency. As you will see later, what tools you include will vary according to the circumstances in which you believe you might have to use your gear.

Anyone who has been in either a genuine or simulated survival situation will know that it is a physically and mentally demanding experience. Making fire using friction methods, creating cordage from natural materials, navigating using the sun or stars, and many other primitive survival tasks are possible, and learning them is an essential part of training, but some take a lot of time and energy, and/or rely on favourable weather and materials, so they are not things you would choose to do in a real situation if you could have easier and more reliable options.

The contents of your PSK will inevitably be limited in size and range of items but will give you an edge that provides a massive boost to morale and resilience to exhaustion when you are trying to carry out what would usually be simple tasks, but without useful tools would now be seemingly impossible because you are mentally numb and physically shaking from cold and fear and tiredness and the trauma of loss.

However, a kit is only any use if you have it with you when it is needed. When a disaster strikes, whether it is a terrorist attack in a city, or a fall while canoeing or crossing a river, or any other major event, you are likely to lose or have to abandon any bag you are carrying as you struggle through crowds and over rubble or try to stay afloat in deep, fast moving water. For it to be with you when you desperately need it, a survival kit must be worn or carried on or very near to the body, never in a pack or bag.

That usually means it has to be compact and sometimes, especially if you are wearing city clothes or uniform, discrete. Your circumstances might require you to carry or wear it hidden, or maybe you can have it in plain sight but not obvious to the untrained eye as to its contents and purpose.

If appearance isn't so critical, then in addition to the basic set you might be able to carry a few extra on-the-body items. Depending on where you live and work or what activities you are undertaking, the laws relevant to that place, and how you dress, these could include a pocket knife or multi-tool, a lighter, a packet of tissues, and a torch, plus a mobile phone with many apps and a wallet or purse with cash. There might be much more but both those and other items fall into the category of Every Day Carry/Every Day Use (EDC/EDU), or basic outdoor equipment, and go beyond the scope of this book. They would also only be relevant if, like the PSK, they were constantly attached to you rather than carried in a bag of any kind. There are full details of that level of equipment and more, and its application, in my book Bugging Out.

For now, let's have a look at some of the options for your Personal Survival Kit.

Choices, choices!

Methods of carry
The traditional PSK followed a military concept of a collection of emergency use items in a small tin. In the UK the container was usually a 2oz tobacco tin and in the USA the even smaller Altoids mint tin. Now the choices have widened into a variety of containers and methods of carry.

Commercial kits can be had in tins, plastic boxes, pouches, or bags wrapped in paracord to be worn as a necklace, pendant, belt, or wristband/bracelet. You can fasten the paracord with buckles – some with extra features such as fire starters or whistles – shackles, clips or sliding toggles. The cord is available in almost any colour you can imagine and many different weave designs. Anyone who makes their own can follow the same path or use a combination of different styles.

In essence, it really doesn't matter. A tin can serve as a pot for collecting and boiling water or cooking, but you could include a piece of baking foil to make a more realistically sized pan, and some of the other kit containers are more watertight. Splitting the contents of your kit among several containers of differing types and means of carry can minimise the size of each, which can give extra security against the loss of it all and make them both more convenient and easier to blend into everyday wear. Because of the size and shape of some kit items they will fit better into some types of container than others.

The wristband/bracelet, for example, can cover a tube or wrap of gear but because of the way it curves around the wrist each item within it must be either small or flexible. A couple of larger items can be integrated as parts of the buckle or worn on the outside, such as a watch or compass. On the other hand, a pouch carried in an inner pocket, or worn on the belt, or at your side between waist and ribs on a cross-body strap under a shirt, will keep your items together for easier transfer when changing clothes and might allow a couple of slightly larger items to be included without causing the kit to become too bulky.

For pouches Maxpedition or Protec have both good reputations and range of sizes (1). I have Maxpedition Micro, mini and EDC – smallest upwards – but they do larger ones too. I find the Micro good for local EDC, the others better depending on how far away or for how long I'm travelling. They come with small carry handles but I cut mine and sewed the 2 halves to form loops for attaching a cross body strap with a buckle near the pouch at the front for easy release if required. A bigger model, or a runner's belt like the FinBurst might suit you better.

Whichever forms you choose, they must fit into how you wear things for the activities you are undertaking or the places you work and travel through, and your personal preferences. As part of my PSK I routinely replace any shoe laces and tie cords on clothing with suitably coloured paracord, since it weighs nothing extra and will always be there without my having to think about it, but I dislike wearing anything around my neck or dangling loose on the outside of clothing. That's due to my experiences of having had them catch on things in dense woodland or while struggling through wrecked buildings, then either hindering my movement or tearing away and being lost. I therefore prefer to wear survival packets close against the sides or back of my body and inside clothes.

Nor am I a great follower of fashion, so bracelets and the like are not the norm for me but, considering my other choices, a paracord wristband containing some PSK pieces when I'm in the wilds, or a similar belt at any time, does make a lot of sense, provided when I use parts of it I keep at least enough to hold my trousers up and keep my shoes tied! Alternatively, instead of one made of paracord, you could choose a money belt and use its pockets in the same way for discrete carry.

Effectively, you have many choices. Just make sure that what you decide on will encourage you to have the kit with you, not tempt you to leave it behind 'just this once' because of its size or colour or style; because sure as Murphy made a law, the 'once' you do leave it behind will be exactly the time you need it most.

Selecting contents
After you've decided what types of containers and how to carry them will most suit you, how do you then decide what to put in them?

The essentials for life remain the same whatever environment you are in: clean air, shelter, warmth, water, food, medical care, and possibly the ability to call for help, to navigate, and to protect yourself. What your local environment does affect is the threats to your access to those essentials and the priorities and methods in which those threats can be addressed.

For example, a container in which to collect, purify and carry water is an important feature for survival in remote areas, so a Ziploc bag or a condom is usually included in a PSK for those areas for that purpose. On the other hand, in urban areas there wouldn't be many places where you couldn't soon find an abandoned plastic soft drink bottle to use as your water container, though you might want to sterilise it before use. Similarly, baking foil has many uses including for making a cooking or water boiling pan but around populated or well travelled areas you shouldn't have to search for long to scavenge an empty food or drink can that would serve as well or better; so while foil might be a feature of a wilderness kit, whether you give room in your urban PSK to that or to something else instead is something for you to consider.

Then again, regardless of if you are lost in the mountains or in a city devastated by a bomb with the consequent destruction of direction signs and familiar landmarks, being able to maintain your line of travel towards an area of greater safety would always make a small compass a very useful aid.

As we review the individual types of tool that you might want to feature in your kit, you should have more information on which to base your selections. However, personal considerations on which I can't make recommendations are also important e.g. if you have a medical ailment for which you need a regular prescription dosage, your PSK must include several days supply in a suitable container, or if you have difficulties with your vision you might want to include a spare pair of contact lenses or folding spectacles. These are personal matters on which you are the best judge and must make your own decision, though also including a copy of your prescription would be a good idea, just in case you found a possible source from which to resupply.

Commercial kits

A few commercial kits contain a sensible collection of good quality items that form a sound foundation on which to build your own PSK. Nevertheless, all are commercial and are built to the designer's ideas and to meet a viable price range for the intended customers, so any of them will need at least some customisation to match your individual needs and preferences. None of them is perfect, many have similar faults that would actually be easy to rectify, and some are quite simply rubbish!

Some miss out whole categories of vital needs, such as including no way to gather, carry, or purify water. Some include low quality items, such as a knife that won't take a decent edge and is so loosely constructed it is dangerous, or a compass that doesn't work at all. Many have common faults, like fish hooks that are too big for anything other than sea or trophy fishing and sinkers that would weigh down a battleship (OK, slight exaggeration, but not by much!).

The fact that some have a NATO Stock Number means that at least one example has at some time been officially purchased, possibly just for evaluation, not that they are accepted military issue items nor that they are in current use by any military force of any NATO country. So please, do not be mislead by advertising blurb into thinking that these kits, or individual items that have a NSN, must be good for you to use because they have a military connection. Even if something is a military stock item, the fact that savvy service personnel will buy an alternative, rather than using the equivalent issue piece, is a good indication that not all are considered 'good kit'. Some kits or items will indeed be of proven worth and may be on general or special issue - the British brass button compass comes to mind - but are expensive, so look for reviews online or in other reliable references and, as always, it is Buyer Beware when it comes to PSKs and individual survival equipment items in general.

The Doug Ritter kits from Adventure Medical Kits contain good quality items and are available from a couple of suppliers in UK but they are rather expensive. You could buy parts, such as the Ritter Mk5 survival knife, separately and then source most of the other items elsewhere and put together an equivalent, but more customised, kit for much less money.

The mini kits from Polymath Products contain a decent selection of good quality items at a fair price – though as usual the fish hooks are too big and you would not want the tiny whistle as your only signalling device when hill walking. The mini tin kit is an excellent starting point for an urban kit because of its small size but a few changes in content will improve it for that environment. The shotgun cartridge style Ultra Compact and Fire Starter kits from the same firm are excellent emergency kits for shooters in wild areas but their looking like a cartridge could generate unwelcome attention among other groups of people or from the authorities if carried in town.

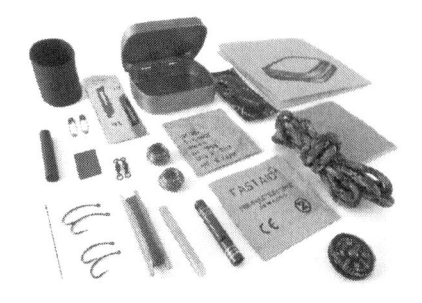

The paracord 'grenade' and wristband kits from The Friendly Swede are good quality at a fair price but are not and are not intended to be complete kits; they contain emergency items that extend a standard set of outdoors equipment.

It would be unfair for me to name individual items or firms to avoid (besides which it could be a very long list!) but, as a general rule, if the name contains the words, 'Ultimate', 'Complete' or 'Military', then it is almost certainly none of those things. So what do you include in a kit?

Wilderness and Military
Wilderness and military kits are aimed at outdoor survival in a wide range of situations, though for extreme environments more specific sets are appropriate. The military kits might accept some weight and bulk in exchange for ruggedness, and include or omit items based on tactical and escape and evasion requirements but in civilian emergencies, although rescue will sometimes be your first choice, in others it is better for anyone to avoid

attracting attention, so tactical features might suit you too.

Remember that you might have lost or had to abandon any bag you had and will now be left with only what you are wearing and your PSK, possibly but not definitely including items that were in the pockets of your outer clothing. I mention that from having seen people who have fallen into deep water or been caught in fire abandon their jackets and even their trousers in order to escape. Your PSK must, therefore, provide for or give a realistic way of creating or acquiring all the essentials for life listed earlier.

Outdoors clothing is generally more rugged and less fashion centred than city wear, so you might get away with carrying rather more kit than you would in the urban setting but it will still be limited by practicality.

If you are actually involved in outdoors activities in the UK, and some other countries, you also have lawful reason for possession of some items, such as a knife, that might be banned in other places or circumstances. However, do be aware of other regulations. For example, in Scotland there are now laws on carrying snares or the wire for making them unless you have the appropriate licence. The chances of you being searched for such equipment, or prosecuted if you had and used it in a genuine emergency, are remote but having and practising with it without authorisation while training could cause you problems.

With those things in mind, what might you include in your PSK?

Cutting tool: even if you carry a folding knife in your pocket or a sheath knife on your belt, a backup cutting tool in your PSK is essential. In the next chapter I discuss the various options in detail but you have the choice of: small fixed blade knife; folding lock knife; folding multi blade knife; mini multi-tool; survival tool with sharp edge; sharpened hacksaw blade; Stanley knife blade; scalpel or craft knife blade; or single edge razor blade, among others.

Each has its pros and cons and some of the simple blade types are small enough that you could include several. It's your choice!

Saw: You can get by without a saw in your PSK; I don't use them for cutting firewood but I do find one to be a useful piece of kit when improvising tools and cutting wood for making shelters.

You can choose from: a length of hacksaw blade; a credit card sized survival tool; a piece of compact wood saw blade or a folding saw with handle; or a wire saw, which is a favourite in PSKs.

Cordage: If you carry a bundle of paracord, use it to replace laces or draw cords, or wear it wrapped around parts of your PSK, then you have your cordage needs covered. Genuine 550lb breaking strain paracord is widely available but 350lb with 5 or 7 inner cords is strong enough for most uses and is more suited to some wrapped or woven kits because it is thinner and more flexible. Otherwise, Kevlar cord or dental floss are very compact options.

Fire starters:

Lighters are invaluable. A piezo ignited butane lighter, carried close to the body in cold weather, is an easy and reliable fire starter but a mini Bic lighter will often fit in a kit if a full size lighter takes too much space. Clipper lighters also use butane but have a flint sparker though they do have one useful feature; the whole sparker unit can be lifted out and the unit used to make sparks for igniting tinder – when available - rather than the fuel in the lighter

Matches still have their place, provided you keep them and their striker surface dry. Strike anywhere types avoid the problem of a wet or worn striker board; lifeboat matches are waterproof, wind resistant and long burning.

Ferrocerium rods are the darling of the Bushcraft crowd but they do only provide a spark which then has to be turned into flame. If mounted on a Magnesium block, however, they provide both sparks and a large source of very hot burning ignition material.

A Fresnel lens is a flat, usually rectangular, plastic magnifying lens which can ignite suitable tinder, or you could try any other magnifying lens, such as one from your glasses or a camera or binoculars, when the weather is good.

Tinder: If you want to make fire from sparks then you need to carry some initial tinder. There is a wide variety available and I will cover these in detail in the chapter on making fire.

Water collection and purification: After shelter and warmth, the next priority in your survival needs is clean water.

Depending on the environment you might be able to collect water in liquid form from a stream or water soaked ground or rain, or you might have to soak up dew or steam if the available ground water is salty or heavily contaminated. After water is collected you will probably need to purify it, which often requires 2 steps: filtration to remove as much suspended matter as possible and then disinfection to kill any remaining bugs. Depending on the size of your PSK, you could carry a cloth filter, such as a Millbank bag, or paper filters such as those used for coffee.

After the water is filtered, chemical sterilisers, such as chlorine or iodine tablets will work more effectively. Potassium Permanganate was a popular choice for water purification at one time. It has fallen from favour because Chlorine tablets are simpler but does have advantages too.

One piece of gear you could have in your PSK is a purification straw. These perform the roles of collection, filtration and purification in a convenient and easy to use form. They are not generally expensive and are lightweight and quite thin but might be too long for your on-the-body kit unless you have or add a narrow pocket of sufficient length.

Your kit could also hold a length of aluminium foil, such as heavy duty baking foil, which you can form into a pan in which to boil water.

Tin opener: If you have a tin opener on your cutting tool then you probably don't need a separate one in a wilderness kit, though military personnel might want one for tins from the 4 or 10 man ration packs. If anyone doesn't have one on another item then I'd include one. Although it is less likely to be used than in an urban area, there are bothies and holiday cabins around in remote areas where in an emergency you might find tinned foods.

Brass or steel wire: Wire has multiple uses in a kit including: shorting a battery to start a fire, making snares, fishing traces, trip lines, binding shelter poles/tools/spears or arrow heads, repairing shoes/packs/clothes, or many of the other uses of cordage. Brass wire is the most commonly used in PSKs because it is easy to handle and if necessary break or cut, versatile and weather resistant, but thin soft steel wire is also sometimes used. The brass wire is usually much thinner than the steel and as such it is better for fishing traces or making snares for birds or small game such as squirrels, but for anything larger you need to use multiple strands. A single strand of steel wire is usually sufficient for rabbits and if you have enough then it could be woven to trap deer or other large game but it is often too thick for fishing and excessive for some binding jobs.

Arrow heads: A relatively recent arrival on the survival scene has been survival cards that include one or more arrow heads attached by a couple of small tabs so that they can be easily broken out. These are flat, well pointed and barbed but not usually sharpened on the edges. It is unlikely that you would go to the effort of making a bow for hunting or defence unless you expected your survival situation to become long term or seriously aggressive, so whether to give space and weight allowance to arrow heads is a consideration.

Fishing kit: Far less controversial is whether to include some fishing tackle. Some kits feature almost everything except a rod and reel but for survival fishing all you really need is hooks, line and sinkers. You can usually find live bait but an artificial fly, maggots or worm don't take up much space or add much weight so you might consider them. There is more on survival fishing later in the book.

Duct tape: or Gorilla tape or service issue black or green tape or any other heavy duty sticky binder. Wind a few feet around your lighter or any other plastic or metal object. Tape is good for repairs to clothing, spectacles and many other things, use as cordage for bindings, securing wound dressings, masking a torch to reduce the light signature, and so much else.

Rubber bands: Wide rubber bands cut from inner tubes can be used to seal survival containers, as part of traps, to power a catapult, to improve your grip on metal or other slippery objects, to provide a safe cover for holding metal things that might get freezing cold, temporary repairs to many tools, or holding stuff together e.g. strapping a PSK container to a belt. The rubber also burns hot but with heavy smoke as a form of tinder.

Button or other small compass: there are many types and makes of button compass on the market and quality varies widely. Good quality dry compasses, such as the UK issue brass button compass or the US EDC brass button compass available from **www.edcgear.co.uk** are the stars but there are many others available.

The Explorer liquid filled compass in 14 or 20mm size (1) or the CountyComm Navigator with rotatable bevel are usually OK. All are available from **www.edcgear.co.uk** among other suppliers.

If you are willing to give a bit more room in your kit to your compass then the Silva 28 Carabiner or Suunto carabiner compass – with the carabiner removed in either case – are reliable and accurate models.

In the chapter on navigation there is detailed information on how to make best use of a button compass

Paper and pencil with eraser: A couple of sheets of waterproof paper and a pencil are useful for making your own map of a stage of any journey, or notes of compass bearings and distances. If you have a pencil with an eraser then when that part of the march is completed you can erase the map and notes and reuse the paper for the next phase. If you have to sharpen the pencil, save the shavings to use as tinder. If you are really desperate then the rubber eraser will also burn.

Torch: In the wilds a powerful and reliable but compact torch is a great asset. Fortunately there are now plenty of choices that meet the need. Go for an LED model with adjustable output but a high top level of brightness for when you need it.

Mini glow sticks: these little light sticks are usually available from fishing tackle suppliers. They have the advantages of being operable in almost all weather, temperature and pressure conditions, are relatively long lasting, compact and light weight. They are not as bright as even the smallest of most torches and are one-time activation but even so, they do have many good uses. There's much more about these in the chapter on lighting.

Whistle: together with a torch, a whistle is classic wilderness emergency signal equipment. One with an output of over 100 decibels is what you are looking for. None of them is expensive and they are quite compact.

Medical items: a strip of adhesive dressing in a sterile cover, an antiseptic or alcohol wipe or two, some pain killers, and any personal medical needs should all be included in your kit. It isn't going to replace a full first aid pack but it should be enough to treat blisters or minor cuts. These can be supplemented with the tampons and duct tape and various other items from your PSK as needed.

Sewing kit: Two strong needles with large eyes that can

take dental floss/Kevlar cord/paracord inner strands should be stored ready threaded in a piece of card with the thread wound around it. One needle with white thread and the other with black covers most needs but if you want full tactical then go for all black or replace the white with green or brown. Add at least 2 safety pins; 1 medium and 1 large.

Urban
A disaster in an urban area, whether from natural causes such as an earthquake, tornado or flood, or manmade due to a bomb or industrial catastrophe, can create an environment in which survival is as traumatic, difficult and challenging as any in the most remote of wildernesses.

The immediate dangers and the resources available to you will not be the same as in the wilds, but the physical and psychological demands placed on you are every bit as draining. Some of the tools you will need to overcome them will be similar to those for any survival scenario, others will be different.

You should start by examining how you travel i.e. car, bus, underground, and the nature of the areas you travel through and where you live, work, shop or whatever it is that takes you there. In particular you should look at the size and type of buildings, the landscape including: streets, roads, railways, parks, rivers, canals, and the facilities e.g. public transport, airports, boats, hospitals, military bases, public telephones, stores that stock potentially useful items such as: outdoor clothing and equipment, food, water, medical items, bicycles, etc., and the nature of people in areas you'd have to travel through, Then evaluate the potential threats, their most damaging effects and what tools would help you to overcome them.

The common dangers of urban disaster include: falling masonry, metal and glass; rough and sharply pointed rubble; flooding; fire; exploding fuel and gas; leaking chemicals and sewerage; live electrical cables; and frightened or feral people and animals. Many of the familiar facilities will be unavailable: emergency services will be over-burdened and their contact numbers inoperable; roads will be blocked; mobile phone and internet connections will show no service available – although texts sometimes eventually get through; electricity supplies could be off or broken; water supplies might be contaminated; few shops or public transport will be operating and those that are may be charging high prices, only be able to take cash, and not give change.

Although many buildings might be unsafe, there will be some, or parts of them, that are abandoned but which can still be used for shelter or from which you could scavenge parts from the rubble to make a bivouac. Or you could hide to rest in a stranded vehicle. Wood and various materials from wrecked buildings, furniture or vehicles will be available to start and fuel a fire but bear in mind the dangers of leaking fuel or gas and that light and smoke from a fire will show your position and possession of some useful goods. Apart from the empty containers and junk always scattered around, in the early days after a disaster you can often find useful tools, cooking vessels, full food and drink containers, clothing, cordage, waterproof sheeting, and many other resources.

Taking those items that you need that are part of the detritus with no clear owner is scavenging and unlikely to get any hostile reaction from officials, unlike breaking into places with the deliberate intention of stealing, which is looting and could get you jailed or shot. However, do remember that the more you have, the more of a target you become to other survivors who consider your stash an easier source of supply than hunting around for their own.

If your rest stop, on your own or with a small group, is intended to be a very temporary break during your trek to a place of greater safety, then only collecting what you need for the day or so and collecting more next day while on the move, can be both safer and less of a burden while you travel. If you decide to stay in the disaster zone then collect as much as you can but split it up and hide it well in several caches spread around your area. To some extent, what actions and activities are 'acceptable' to others, and to your own conscience, will depend on the severity of the disaster and the destruction it has caused.

By all means keep in mind the resources that are likely to be available to you, depending on your knowledge and level of skills, but don't assume that everything you want will fall easily to hand when you need it. A PSK is just as useful in this environment as in the woods or moors.

Preppers who envisage using their PSK for getting home from an urban area but then across varied terrain and over a fair distance, often include items from the wilderness kits for use during their travel, but actually for the urban environment, some of the things you might want to include are:

Cash and coins: in some situations, or after you get out of the worst affected area, you might be able to hire transport, make a telephone call, or buy essentials from a shop or vending machine if you have some coins and low denomination notes. Neither electronic tills nor ATMs might be working so your credit and debit cards would not be of any use for payment or getting cash after the event. Having some hard cash on you can make life much easier. How much you choose to carry is entirely up to you but consider what you might use it for and what providers may charge in these events.

Cordage: I routinely replace shoe laces and any jacket draw cords with paracord as a handy source of cordage but you might also decide to use it to cover kits as part of your PSK, including a wristband in a weave and colour(s) that match your style and fashion preference. Alternatively, either dental floss or Kevlar cord is a compact, strong option that is useful for many tasks from tool binding to sewing clothes or flesh, or for cleaning between your teeth but in the urban environment scavenging might give you other choices.

Knife or other blade: If your kit includes a proper knife or multi-tool then you are in luck but because of the law that isn't available to everyone in all urban areas. You might have to go for a smaller blade buried deep in your kit. Have a look at the chapter on cutting tools for the various options.

Fire starters and tinder: As per the comments for Wilderness and Military kits. The choice is yours but you should definitely have at least one or 2, and preferably 3 options. Perhaps the one advantage ferro rods have in an urban area is that dry tinder will probably be easier to find, in the form of stuffing from house and vehicle furniture, first aid kits, etc.

Water purification tablets: even in an urban area when it still comes from a tap or broken domestic water pipe, you can't be sure after a disaster that the clear looking water you are seeing isn't badly contaminated in some way. You might have a container in which you can boil it, if you decide it is safe to make a fire, but purification tablets are so compact and light that it doesn't make much sense not to have some in your PSK so that you have the option. You will want at least 2 litres per day for drinking and perhaps some extra for washing wounds, so I advise at least 6, with 2 strips of 10 being better but, within sensible limits, more is never wrong in this regard.

Tin opener: even if you carry a multi-blade pocket knife or a survival card that has a tin opener as one of the tools, a P-38 or P-51 style folding tin opener is a really handy tool. In an urban area you are far more likely to scavenge tins of food than to be fishing or trapping so an easy way to get into them is an obvious choice.

Brass or steel wire: these have all the same uses as in the wilderness, except that you are less likely to be using them as snares or fishing traces. What you are more likely to do is use a couple of lengths to strike sparks from a rescued car or phone battery in order to start a fire. You might also use it as trip wires or to open car doors or window latches.

Electrical tape: Some electrical tape wound around your kit or on a plastic card within it can be used for improvised electrical connections for light or other facilities, for binding items, to secure a wound dressing, make a temporary repair to torn clothing, or if in a bright colour be used as a position marker or distress signal.

Rubber bands: wide rubber bands – sometimes referred to in survival literature as 'Ranger bands' – can be useful for keeping your tins sealed, making improvised tools and weapons, emergency shoe repairs and as hot-burning durable tinder for fire lighting. You can make your own by cutting strips from bicycle or other inner tubes. Punctured ones that are fine for this use are often available free for asking from bike and car accessory shops.

Hacksaw blade: or as long a piece of one as will fit into your kit. As well as serving as a wood saw and a striker for a ferro rod, you can use it for sawing through hasps that are being secured by padlocks (the metal of the padlock itself will be too hard), or through window frames and locks for entry to or exit from buildings or storage lockers

Mini pry bar: a full sized crow bar or wrecking bar would be better but unlikely to be suitable for discrete carry! There are simple miniature pry bars available and others that feature all sorts of tools such as; bottle opener, spanners, cutting edges, nail pullers, and much more. Do a search online and you will be amazed at some of the things people sell.

Lock picks and bump key: if you are willing to take the time to develop the necessary skills, and to take the chance of being prosecuted for 'going equipped', then as well as amazing your work colleagues who forget their desk or locker keys, you can use these items to give you access to or egress from many places that would otherwise require considerable force and noise.

Chain and padlock: Ladies could wear the chain openly as a fashionable belt, men under their shirt as a rather less fashionable kit hanger or a belt with the chain wrapped in woven paracord. For either, the chain and padlock serves as an effective defensive weapon against 2 or 4 legged aggressors, or can be used to break a window, or to secure a fence or gate behind you if you are being pursued. If you use it as a weapon, be robust; put the attacker down, don't give them a chance to take the chain and turn it against you.

Button compass: even if you are familiar with a town or city it can become disorientating and strange after a disaster. Many of the features you know might have fallen or been defaced and your normal routes made impassable due to rubble, fire, flooding or crashed and abandoned vehicles. A small compass can be a real help in these circumstances.

Paper and pencil with eraser: Good for leaving a note of your intentions somewhere prearranged, in case anyone comes looking for you at your starting point, or for making your own rough maps, or keeping a record of your journey, or use with the compass as a navigation aid (see the detailed instructions for using a button compass).

Marker pen: if you work with a group or have made plans with your family, you could have arrangements to leave coded messages on the back of signposts or as graffiti on walls, to let them know of your progress and direction of travel.

Torch: a pocket torch or even a key ring light can be a real morale booster if you are trapped in a collapsed building or have to travel in unlit urban areas. If you have capacity, spare batteries might be useful but if possible carry one that takes AAA or AA rather than button cells, because they will be easier to find in the wreckage, either new or in abandoned or broken equipment. Otherwise consider a wind-up model; there are some very small torches on sale with good levels of light output.

Mini glow sticks: often available in various colours from places selling fishing gear these are tiny but give off a surprisingly useful amount of light for several hours. They can relieve the horror of complete darkness, give you enough light to read a compass or map, or be left as way markers.

Whistle: If you are trapped and trying to let potential rescuers know where you are, a whistle is a more effective and less tiring signal maker than your voice. If you know proper distress signals, that is great but if not just letting people know you are there and alive is a major bonus.

Medical items: a strip of adhesive dressing in a sterile cover, an antiseptic or alcohol wipe, some pain killers, and any personal medical needs should all be included in your kit. It isn't going to replace a full first aid pack but it should be enough to treat blisters or minor cuts.

Sewing kit: 2 strong needles with large eyes that can take dental floss/Kevlar cord/paracord inner strands should be stored ready threaded in a piece of card with the thread wound around it. Add at least 2 safety pins and you should be able to maintain your clothing sound enough to avoid you frightening the natives and keep out the cold winds.

Mini USB drive or data card: If you have lost access to any bag you normally carry and to access to your car, you might also have lost vital identity documents, driving licence, and other information. In some cases, scans of these documents aren't as acceptable to authorities as the originals, but they are a lot better than nothing at all. The card/drive could also contain a vast library of useful survival information.

Personal photo: whatever equipment you might have,

the most important aid to survival is determination. A photograph of your family or other loved ones can remind you of your reason to go on and reinforce your resolve to survive.

Your particular circumstances could mean that not all of the items in the kits covered are applicable to you, or there might be additional pieces that are, but the lists above should give you a starting point from which to adapt. The lists seem long but – depending on which of some of the options such as knife and pry tool you pick - all of the items will easily fit into a compact kit the size of a tobacco tin or small pouch.

There is more detail on the options and effective use of each of these items in the chapters that follow.

Cutting Tools

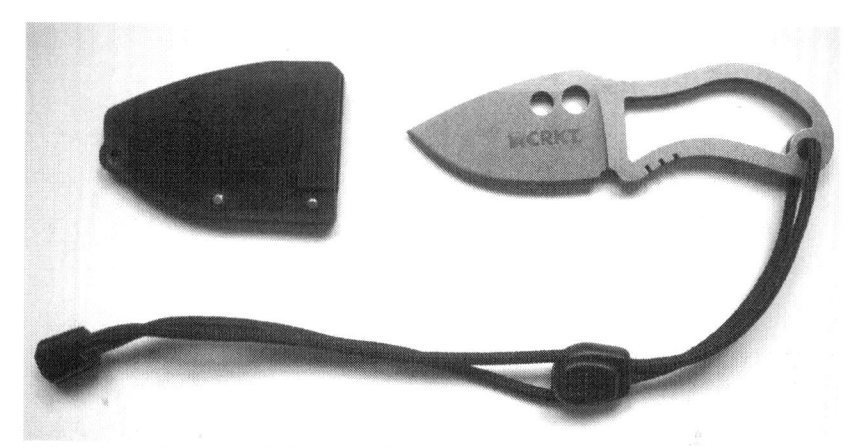

Most outdoor activity enthusiasts agree that a cutting tool is one of the most important pieces of equipment you carry. There are things you can use to improvise in a survival situation e.g. flint or quartz, broken glass, sharpened tin, etc. but this tool is so critical that you won't want to have to improvise if you can possibly avoid it.

Those who can, still carry a UK legal blade in addition to their Personal Survival Kit but legal restrictions or professional dress requirements can limit both the form and size of tool that it is practical to have on your person at all times. Whether for that reason, or as a backup, it is therefore normal to include a cutting tool of some sort hidden away in a PSK.

This book is specifically about things that are practical to include in such a kit so we will leave the knives and tools carried separately for discussion elsewhere and concentrate on the qualities and use of the small tools that most often feature in a tin or pouch.

There are 5 classes of blade that are likely to be included in PSKs: Fixed blade, folding knives, mini multi-tool, card tools, and simple blade. Any of the tools other than the simple blades offer the advantage of increased utility but at the cost of space taken up in a kit. Whether the associated loss of space for other things is justified or not depends on the purpose and expected use of the kit and what other equipment can be carried i.e. is the cutting tool in the kit the primary/only one available or is it a backup.

Fixed blade knives

Fixed blade knives generally offer strength, greater cutting edge length, edge shape, and the improved usability of a proper handle, over the other types of cutting tools in PSKs. Small knives that could be pressed into this role have been around for a long time but recently some have been produced specifically to be included in tin-sized kits.

Perhaps the best known commercial models are: the Doug Ritter RSK Mk5 from CRKT (see the picture at the top of this chapter); the Turley, Latitude 43 and Thumbnail from TOPS; and the NC 1001 and 1002 from Navy; but there are now others and close copies of them being produced by other makers, including a couple from China that I have reviewed.

The RSK Mk5 has an overall length of 9.7cm (3.8") with a blade length of 4.4cm (1.75") and a thickness of 3mm (0.11"). It is made from 3Cr13 stainless steel hardened to 52-55 HRC and weighs 26 grams. It is available in either a stone-washed (grey) or black finish. The point and curve of the blade are useful, with the full cutting edge being 5cm (2") and mine arrived sharp but required a bit of honing to make it shaving-sharp. The handle, at just over 5cm, is only a couple of finger widths long but it does come with a lanyard attached and following the advice in the instruction leaflet on how to use that does improve your grip slightly. It is provided with a push-fit Kydex sheath that seems secure atm. The knife will fit (just!) in an Altoids tin or comfortably in a Tobacco tin.

For its size, the Mk5 has proven very capable. Common

sense will tell you that the size does limit its functionality - it will never replace a big knife or hatchet for chopping heavy branches or splitting logs - but I have used it for making fire materials, trap triggers and various tools, cutting cordage and natural materials to make cordage, slicing Hessian and leather, and cleaning rabbits, squirrels and pigeons. There is a very honest appraisal of the compromises involved in the design and production of the knife, with pictures of it in use, on Doug Ritter's site at: http://www.dougritter.com/rsk_mk5.htm

The Navy 1002 is a different concept. It combines a straight cutting edge, chisel edge and prying notch. The main edge is shorter than that on a single edge razor blade and only about half that of a Stanley knife blade but its advantage is in the thickness/strength at the back, which is similar to that of the RSK i.e. 3mm/0.11". It also takes an edge that is easily the equal of the Stanley knife blade and retains it well in appropriate uses.

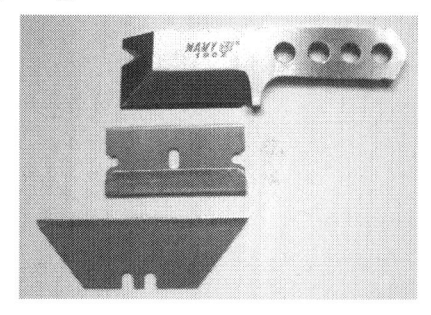

I don't generally like single sided knives (the reverse side of this is completely flat) but it is understandable given the basic design of this tool and, for its purposes, it hasn't proven to be a major disadvantage in use or sharpening, which is easy enough even though edge retention isn't at all bad. The tool comes with a thin leather sheath and price is usually under £10.

There is a newer version, the 1003, which has a point rather than the chisel/prying edge. I haven't handled one of those yet. It is available on Amazon at £12.80 and if I was buying one of these tools I'd go for that rather than the 1002.

*Note: any fixed blade knife is unlawful for UK EDC in a public place unless you can show you have lawful or

reasonable excuse for carrying it

Folding knives

Folding knives in PSKs tend to be one of two types: single blade lock knives or small multi-blade folders.

Lock knives

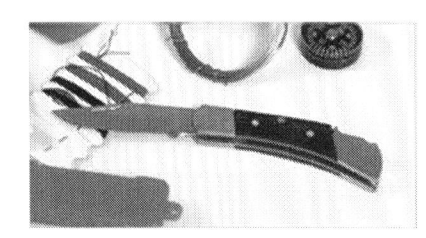

The lock knives in some commercial kits are of decent quality but unfortunately that isn't true in all cases. The first ones with which I came into contact were the miniature Buck knife copies in BCB tin kits. How any responsible company could put something like this into kits upon which someone might rely for survival defies logic!

The ones I tested arrived blunt and refused all my attempts to put a decent edge on them. The grind varied in angle not only from side to side but at various places along the length of the blade. Even after I had reground that to a consistent level, the poor quality of the steel prevented it from taking a fine edge or from keeping in use what it did take. When 'locked' open the blades wobbled both in the lock and from side to side. The fit of the wooden slabs in the handle was appalling.

We always recommend that every user of PSKs should test, become thoroughly familiar with, and replace if necessary, every item in their kit. If you carry something for potential use in a disaster then your life might depend on its quality and your ability to use it. If you pay for something then it should be fit for purpose but it is your responsibility to ensure that is the case. Anyone who doesn't, deserves everything they get!

Just to prove that BCB garbage isn't always representative though, I found a little knife that came in a discounted kit I bought in a sale in Blacks. It is a skeletonised, one-handed opening, 2"-ish cutting edge lock knife which bears the Web Tex label. Somewhat suspicious from previous experiences, I didn't expect much when it slid out of the water bottle type container in which the kit was housed. I've been pleasantly surprised.

It is light but hardy in regular field use. It hones to an excellent edge and keeps it well enough in appropriate uses. It came with an attached pocket clip but I removed that because I wanted to use the knife in compact kits and the clip nearly doubled the thickness. It is a small knife and a locking blade folder, so you aren't going to try to use it to chop down trees but for use on game, light carving, and similar level tasks it performs very well indeed.

It doesn't have a maker's mark, just a 440 Stainless note, so I haven't been able to establish the price or manufacturer, but if you are looking for another solid but very cheap lock-back then try this next one!
http://www.heinnie.com/rough-rider-lockback-stainless
£2.95

That's right, an all stainless, solid, lock knife with a 2.5" blade and a 3" handle, no 'walk' or 'talk' when open, that takes and keeps a shaving edge, for under £3 from Heinnie

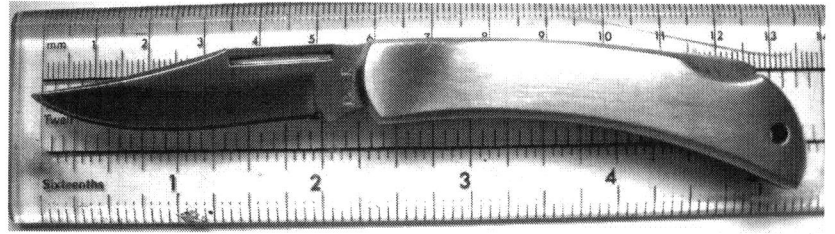

Haynes. The Rough Rider all stainless lock knife might be made in China but it is an excellent example of the quality that they can put out to belie the junk we often see from there. If you are looking for a small pocket knife for

inclusion in a kit then there are some other superb ones – like those from Spyderco, but not at this price.

Small lock knives of good quality offer a compact solution that is safe in use even when the situation and your condition are at dangerously low levels. Like all small knives they have their limits and you should recognise and respect those in the tasks to which you apply them and how you handle them but you could do far worse.

Non-locking folders
However, as with fixed blades, lock knives are great wilderness kit but don't meet the law's requirements, for most people, for EDC in the UK. For that you need a small non-locking folder. There are plenty available from differing manufacturers but for our purposes I don't think you can go wrong with any of the executive or small range from Victorinox.

For a mid-level blade then try the 2-blade Pocket Pal or even the 1-blade Excelsior.

For an even smaller knife but with more facilities then the Classic SD, or any of the other mini knives, is a good option.

These knives offer compact quality and reliability in a lawful form, with good handling and, in some cases, a variety of tools. Even if you can carry a larger pocket knife, they provide a first class backup. With good handling techniques, e.g. cutting away from you and not using undue pressure in a wrong direction while your fingers are wrapped around the handle, the lack of a lock need not put you in harms way. Just think about what you are doing and use common sense in doing it.

Card tools and Mini Multi-tools

Some card tools, like the Victorinox SwissCard or Tool Logic, are pretty much multi-blade penknives with the various components put into a plastic case rather than folding into a frame on end pivots, while others are single pieces of metal with the edges and various holes given different functions. A new version comes in the form of a credit card-sized metal sheet which contains a range of break out items.

Mini multi-tools really are miniature versions - sometimes just smaller, in other cases with fewer or differently designed tools – of the standard multi-tool made famous by Leatherman but now with many competitors from different manufacturers. They differ from multi-blade penknives mainly in that their primary function is not the cutting blade but (usually) pliers or scissors.

Both forms of set offer you tools to carry out differing tasks, some of which might be useful daily but of little relevance in an emergency. Some of the functions, e.g. saw, tin opener, scraping edge, could replace individual kit items with the same purpose and fill the space and weight taken in the kit by them, some might simply be extras. Depending on your approach to the contents of your PSK, you might decide to carry the tool regardless, basically as an EDC item, or to accept the irrelevant items and include it in the PSK, or reject it as taking an unacceptable amount of space and weight for the benefits it offers. You're the one carrying it, so it's your choice!

However, this section of the thread is about Cutting Tools, so regardless of the other features of the various considered devices it is on that function that I will concentrate.

Card tools

Card tools are sometimes included in a PSK, particularly in pouches, but in the case of tins they are often taped, or attached with bands, to the outside. This saves space within the tin while adding very little to its bulk and is practical because the cards and their tools are usually weather resistant.

Multi-tool, plastic sheath cards almost always contain a cutting blade of some sort, though the design and functionality varies considerably. The classic Victorinox SwissCard has a very simple, flat blade and handle extension but despite its simplicity the quality of the steel makes it a very effective cutting tool for its size.

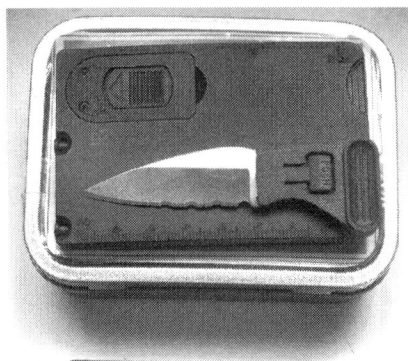

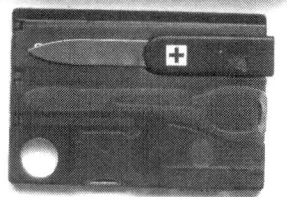

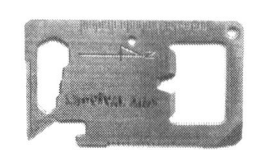

If you are desperate and ready to risk the loss of your cutter, the design makes it adaptable for fitting as a point on an arrow or a slingshot bolt, but my choice is to sharpen the tip of the nail file to use for that purpose. Since we are looking at cutting tools though, we must consider that the SwissCard also has scissors and their use whenever practical and appropriate will help to maintain the sharpness of your main cutting blade.

Tool Logic produces at least 5 card tools with slightly differing blade and handle configurations, as well as differing tool sets. Four have a part serrated cutting edge, one has a gut hook, and all have a quite aggressive sharply pointed blade. I haven't tried the 'Pocket Hunter' with plain blade and gut hook, or the Survival 2, or the tool Lite – though the latter 2 have the same design of knife as the Survival 1 - but I do have the other 2 and both cut and carve well. The blades are strong, the handles small but offer a usable grip. The Survival 1 gives a longer, possibly 2 fingers, grip depending on how fat your fingers are but I prefer that on the Survival Card Companion because I find it handles well in a variety of different holds. In an extreme situation, the design also allows the knife to be gripped with the blade extending forward of the fist.

The fixed blade means these tools breach EDC regulations in UK but elsewhere they would be a good urban choice. The Survival 1 has: whistle, ferro rod, tweezers, tooth pick, magnifying glass and compass; the Companion has tweezers, tooth pick, magnifying glass and compass, tin opener and screwdriver; the others have variations on the above.

There are other makes of tools with similarities and differences from the above, and plenty of copies, but these are fairly representative.

The other type of card tool is well represented by the Survival Aids survival tool. The one in these pictures dates back to the 1980s but there are many newer versions with various differences. Quality varies vastly so, let the buyer beware!

The SA tool has been with me as part of my kit and kits just about everywhere I have been over the years and still has a place in my wallet or bag. It is a capable piece of kit that will carve, shave, saw, open tins and (many!) bottles, strip wire and serve most of its other functions effectively.

The only thing I never did get to work, despite trying every trick I could think of including suspending it in various ways or floating it on wood, cardboard or plastic, was to get it to work as a compass needle, though it is just about magnetic enough on the 'northerly' edge to pick up a sewing needle or other small piece of steel.

As I said, not all tools are equal! The black copy of the SA tool I have came as 1 of 2 items in a special deal for £4.99, so I suppose I shouldn't judge it too harshly. It will shave fuzz curls, open tins and bottles, undo nuts from bolts, etc. but when it comes to sawing, well, if you persist you might get it to rub a shallow groove into wood before you eventually decide you'd be better gnawing it with your own teeth!

Mini Multi-tools
While card tools are often fastened to the outside of PSKs, if mini multi-tools are to be considered a part of one then they really have to go inside; otherwise they go on a key ring or whatever and become a separate part of everyday or emergency equipment. Including them in the kit is fine if you are going with a slightly larger kit such as a pouch or mini mess tin but in smaller kits appropriate for EDC their inclusion really does become debateable considering the other items that then have to be omitted. The more functions they have, the more versatile they are, but the larger they become so the essentialness, utility and desirability of each item have to be carefully considered.

In addition to size, you also have to consider quality and while some manufacturers turn out tools that are very good others are absolute dross and, frankly, would not be worth pack room if instead of walking you were riding an elephant and leading a caravan of camels! Unfortunately that is particularly true when considering multi-tools with regards to their cutting tools. Since they are not the primary function, lower quality tools in particular often don't give them the importance that they deserve.

Let's have a look at some of what is available and what they really offer as part of a PSK.

Starting at the very top of the line, we have the entries from Leatherman. The two most appropriate current models for these purposes are the Micra and the Squirt.

The main tool of the Micra is actually a cutting tool, though scissors rather than the knife. I have found them to be sharp and robust and have even used them to open a rabbit and remove the feet after breaking the joint.

They do need to be kept clean and very lightly lubricated to stop them becoming stiff after a while but overall they are very good. The knife blade is small. It takes a reasonable edge, has a useful point and belly contour but does need frequent resharpening if used on hard wood. The remainder of the features are of questionable value in an emergency, though in an urban area you might possibly use the small screwdrivers.

The main feature of the Squirt is pliers but it has a similar knife to the Micra and much smaller but still good quality scissors. The file is short but actually useful. The screwdrivers are similar to those on the Micra.

Reviews and reports on both tools differ as to production quality on varying features and also on the durability. I haven't had any problems with my Micra but any question on reliability of a tool intended for emergency use is a concern. Customer service from Leatherman in regard to problems with their tools receives excellent reports but that doesn't help you in times when you absolutely need something to work and it doesn't.

Features on tools from different manufacturers vary, with some being more oriented to outdoor use rather than cosmetic maintenance but whether you look at those from

Gerber or Rolson, SOG, Wilkinson or True Utility, reliability in hard use is often suspect, as should really be expected from small items designed for ease of carry and intended for lighter work.

As an example, I have 2 from True Utility. One is a Scarab and the other is the TU242 Micro Tool. The scarab (or a copy) is included in the BCB Ultimate survival kit and after extensive testing I have to say I don't have a much better opinion of it than I do of the lock knife included in the earlier kits. The tips of the pliers don't meet when in use because of where they do further down, the wire cutters are ok but only on the thinnest of wire, the knife blade is smaller than some of the scalpel blades I review in the next part of this chapter but came too blunt to scratch anything let alone cut it. It has sharpened somewhat after a lot of work but I wouldn't give it a second thought as a potential PSK cutting tool compared to anything else I've looked at. The edges and tips of the screwdrivers are rounded so they don't bite well in any of the screws I've tried and I've yet to think of a survival use for the nail cleaner/file.

The MicroTool has a slightly better blade and arrived with a reasonable edge that responded more quickly to honing, plus a pair of scissors that are tiny but do cut. It has the same useless nail file/cleaner as the Scarab plus a bottle opener with file extension. The tool has the virtue of compactness and on first inspection it seems reasonably well made but if I wanted to carry it I'd cut back the screwdriver to a small projection beyond the front of the bottle opener and file/grind the opener to make it function as a tin opener too.

When prompted, I tried the nail file for a couple of alternative uses and in fact you can light a strike-anywhere match on it, it will spark a ferro rod and it will – very slowly – file powder from a magnesium block, but a piece of hacksaw blade is better for any of those functions.(1)

Over all, I can see why some people would carry the mini tools as part of EDC kit, particularly for light everyday use as opposed to dedicated emergency applications. However, if you want to dual-purpose one then you need to choose carefully, test thoroughly, and have backup tools or procedures in mind, which considering that these items are often carried as backups seems rather odd.

Simple blades

The final category of cutting tool found in PSKs is the simple blade. There might be some I've missed, or decided not to bother with – such as pencil sharpener and small craft knife blades – because they are too similar to others in the list, but these five are fairly representative of what you will most often find in various sizes of commercial or home-made kits.

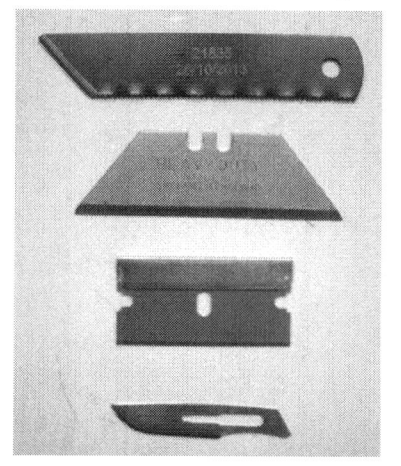

The five are: sharpened hacksaw blades, scalpel blades, Stanley knife blades, single-sided razor blades, and the Sharp Eye.

Hacksaw blades

Hacksaw blades are usually included in a PSK as a striker for a Ferrocerium rod but sometimes also serve in military or urban kits as an Escape and & Evasion tool. However, the temper of the steel also means that many will take a sharp cutting edge to go with the saw teeth. Some are ground or filed to provide a point while others have notches or barbs for use on arrows.

Probably the simplest are similar to the sharpened blade from the ubiquitous BCB Ranger fire steel set. On the Ranger hacksaw the forward edge can be sharpened on one side to provide a chisel type blade or on both sides to provide a more classic knife blade. This can be honed to shaving level or given a more robust angle for less precision but greater durability. I prefer the extra sharpness for the tasks for which I expect to use the blade but if you are using it to produce shavings from a magnesium block, for example, the longer lasting edge is more appropriate.

If you want to get fancier, and have room in your kit for a longer piece of hacksaw blade, then you could go with one of the designs from the m4040.com site or others that are similar.

http://www.m4040.com/Survival/DollarSurvivalKnife/Dollar_Survival_Knife.htm

The simple but multi-purpose features of a flat, space-miserly, sharpened hacksaw blade are attractive options in any small kit. Even if you decide on a different blade type as your main cutting tool, this is a useful extra that adds no additional bulk or weight (in fact it marginally reduces both) for the cost of just a few minutes work with a grinder or file and sharpening stones.

Scalpel blades

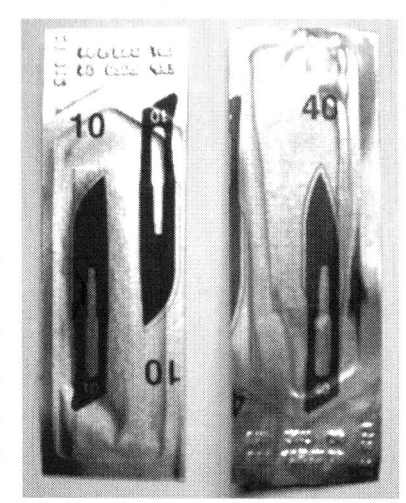

Scalpel blades are usually provided as the cutting tool as a space saving option in very small kits but are also sometimes included as an extra among the medical items in larger ones. They have the advantage of extreme sharpness

but the disadvantages of a less durable edge and difficulty in handling safely, at least when straight from the packet.

The most common type provided seems to be the #10 but there are many available in differing styles and sizes. Different sizes or shapes might serve your intended uses better than the #10 and most are usually available for just a couple of pounds for 10.

The difficulty in safe usage can be resolved, if you have room in your kit, by adding a commercial handle. If the handle is slightly too long, as they are for tobacco or Altoids tins, you can resolve that in a few minutes by use of a hacksaw to reduce the handle's length and then a file to round it off.

If you don't have room in the kit for a handle then you

can always improvise one. It takes just a stick, a blade and some binding material from your kit. For the one in the picture, I broke a stick from a fallen pine branch and cut it to length. I then cut/scraped a notch into what would be the underside of the handle, making the cut just long and deep enough to take the tang of the blade, while leaving the top edge of the stick intact. I pushed in the blade – taking care to handle it by the back – and then bound it tightly in place. Job done!

The binding took only a couple of feet of the dental floss that I often include as cordage in mini kits, due to its strength to weight/bulk ratio. I could also have used the Kevlar thread, inner strands of paracord, or tape that have a place in various kits. The fixing is firm and tight and makes the blade much easier to use safely and effectively. A similar method works for attaching blades to shafts as arrow points.

Stanley knife blades and single edge razor blades

Stanley knife blades are generally larger and easier to handle in their bare form than scalpel blades and they have a longer cutting edge, allowing for more extended effective cutting time or a longer cutting stroke. They still benefit from a handle but because they do not have a tang like that on a scalpel blade the method of fitting them has to differ slightly and it takes a bit more work.

Single edge razor blades are basically the same format but with a thickened rear edge. They are smaller than the Stanleys, sharper, but less durable. Fitting and using handles is very similar.

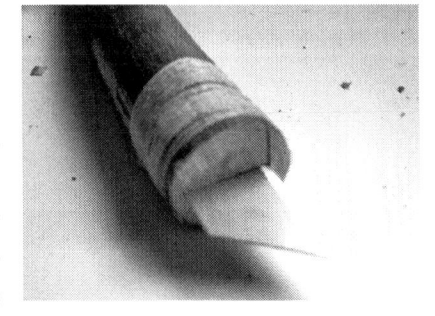

I start with a thicker piece of wood, with enough depth to fully enclose the height of the blade plus about 50% and cut it to a square end. Taking into consideration the grain of the wood, I measure the length of the blade that I want to enclose and mark that point on the underside of the handle. I then baton in the blade across the stick to create a cut at that point, to a depth that will provide for the slice I am going to remove. Ensuring that there is sufficient wood at the back of the stick to support the blade when cutting, I then remove a slice of wood from the underside. After fitting the blade this will be replaced to prevent the blade edge from cutting the binding material.

Using the hacksaw blade from my kit, and ensuring I retain the integrity of the back of the stick, I then cut a slot from the end of the stick back to the same length as the removed slice. I then fit the blade, replace the slice and bind the whole thing with whatever binding material I have available.

I kept this one simple but, depending on your intended uses, you can adjust the length of blade that is exposed and could taper the sides of the handle from the back of the blade to where it emerges, in order to make it easier to manipulate and for you to observe exactly where you are making the cut. If you want to use the blade for shaving rather than slicing you could also simply cut a notch into the front of the handle and push in the blade leaving the whole of the cutting edge exposed. I try to make the slot as tight as possible but also tap in a tiny wedge to firm it up even more. That works but do try to centre your push on the centre line of the blade to prevent it tipping sideways in the handle.

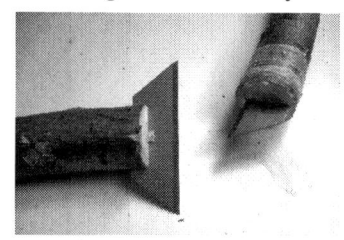

Sharp Eye

Unique, as far as I know, to The Friendly Swede range of kits, the Sharp Eye is a ferro rod striker washer with a serrated edge plus an extension that is sharpened as a cutting edge.

The serrated edge is not intended for cutting but for scraping or shaving a ferro rod or magnesium block but I have also found it very

43

effective for shaving curls from wood to form feather sticks.

The cutting edge on all of the Sharp Eyes I have received has been extremely sharp and often wrapped in tape to prevent it cutting the paracord wrapping of the wristband and 'grenade' kits in which it is usually sold, though one is also included in the paracord craft kit from TFS, along with 3 colours of cord, ferro rods, and various buckles and shackles.

The first one I tried came as part of a wristband 'fishing and fire' kit sold as the Multi-purpose Paracord Wristband Survival Kit for Preppers (£10.99 from Amazon UK). After using the kit to catch a fish I tried the sharp eye blade to gut it and was impressed by the fast, clean cutting stroke. I used it for multiple cutting tasks after that, and started a fire to bake the fish, using an edge of the washer part to spark the ferro rod to ignite the feather sticks I had made with the serrated edge.

It's an unusual, versatile and effective little piece of kit and I have included one in several of the kits I have made.

A Sharpening stone that is small enough to fit in the kit is also extremely useful. You can use many fine-grained natural stones to help remove serious burrs from a knife edge but few of them will really give a sharp hone to it. You can whet what edge you have using glass, metal or a piece of ceramic ware, if you can find one, but if you have room then a proper honing tool is worth its place.

Saws

A small saw can be a valuable tool in either a wilderness or urban PSK. In urban areas particularly it can help to gain access to storage cupboards or through fences, doors or windows. In any environment, considering that your cutting tool might be restricted to a small simple blade, they are also good for cutting grooves and notches in wood, plastic or metal when making tools, trap triggers, or weapons such as bows and arrows, spears or catapults.
There are various forms that might suit your needs.

Pocket chain saws

For most pocket kits these are both a bit too big and too aggressive in their cutting and they are restricted to sawing wood but if you routinely travel through remote, heavily forested areas you might consider one. They will effectively cut much thicker and harder timber than any of the other types but do add weight and bulk in your kit.

There are several variations available from differing suppliers or you can make your own.

The first of the 2 I'll show here is fairly typical of the commercial models; the Ultimate Survival SabreCut saw from Ultimate Survival Technologies.

This one came in an 'Ultimate Survival Kit' but the saw is also now available separately. The kit is expensive at around £70 but the contents are generally high quality. Just the saw with a pouch is nearly £30. Alternative models run from about £7 upwards but, as you might guess, quality varies widely.

I have found this saw to be tough and extremely effective and most other reviews report similar results. No doubt you could break it if you really tried but with sensible use it is a very practical piece of kit. Because of the size however, mine is part of my vehicle kit rather than included in a PSK.

The second saw is one I made from a standard chainsaw chain.

I simply filed the top off one of the rivets and tapped it out, fitted a couple of key rings through the resulting holes and then attached tape wrist loops to those. It is even more aggressive than the SabreCut, though it requires a bit more effort in the cutting stroke, and was half the price. It is also about half as long again, which can be an advantage or hindrance, depending on the location where you are cutting and the position you have to adopt. Generally though, it is quite impressive in use.

Wire saws

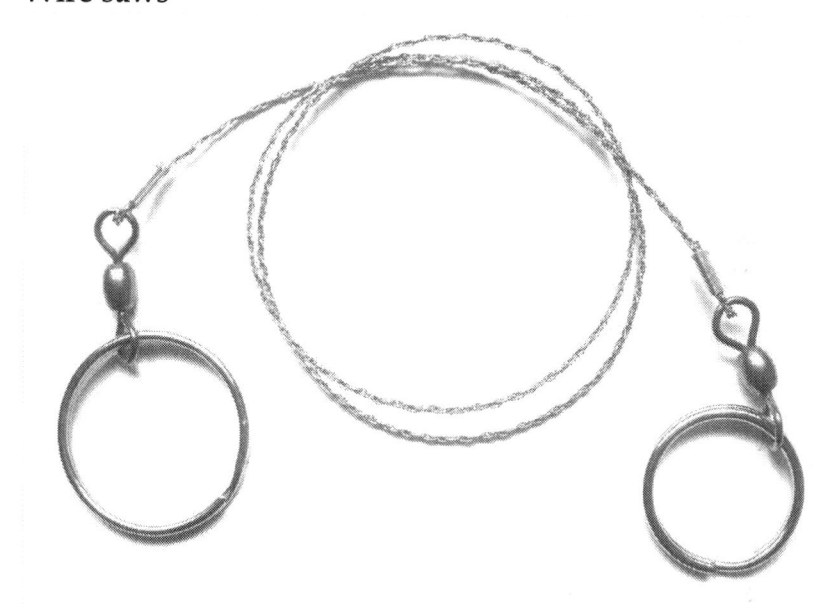

The very early wire saws tended to be poor quality and not very effective, having an edge more like a file than a true saw. Quality of current models also varies, particularly in strength of the wire used, but good ones are a viable tool, if they are used properly!

The saw in the picture above is an M.O.D. issue model. Inevitably suppliers and features change over time but the distinguishing features of these are: brass swivels, a different size of steel ring at each end one of which will fit through the other, and strong clamps holding the folded wire, though I believe the current issue model has nylon tape wrist loops rather than rings.

Poorer quality models tend to have same-sized flat-sided split rings, silver coloured swivels, inferior clamps on the wire and a noticeably less sharp feel when you run your fingers along them. The wire in some is also stiffer than on the good ones.

The key to using these saws effectively is to ensure the wire is flat and tight when cutting. This can be done by keeping your hands wide apart, though that isn't easy, or by having a person on each end of the saw or by fitting the saw to a bent branch to form a bow saw. How springy a branch and how much curve you will need on it will be dictated by the thickness of the wood you need to cut but for tools, traps, etc. something like that shown is adequate; if you are cutting logs for a cabin then you should really be using a different tool!

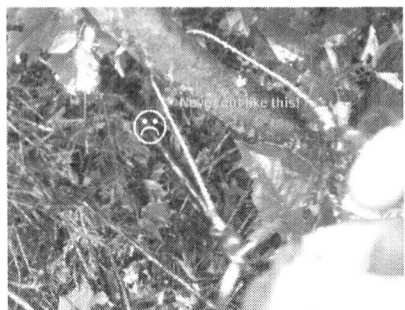

Never make the mistake of curling the wire around the wood and pulling quickly with your hands close together. It seems efficient but you will almost certainly overheat the wire and cause it to break. A tight wire and slow, steady cutting strokes is always the way to go.

If you do get over-enthusiastic and break the wire, don't discard it! Even though the cutting length will be shorter and large tasks will take longer, it is often possible to fold the broken end of the longer piece of wire around the other swivel or ring and bind it with a piece of snare wire. Obviously the result isn't as good as the original but it is usually better than no saw.

Pocket folding saws

There are many folding saws on the market but not many could realistically be classed as a 'pocket' saw. Opinel make a couple of excellent models but even the smallest is based on their no.12 frame - which is the biggest for their range of folding knives - and at 16.4cm/6.5" long folded it is too big for even most pouch based PSKs

The Tops Pocket Saw, at 12cm/4.75" will 'just' fit diagonally into a tobacco tin kit. It has an effective though finely toothed blade and is both light and flat for its size.

I like it enough that one has a place in my shooting bag for making hides and since adopting it I've never wished I had something bigger for that role. I also have one in a cross-body pouch kit for wild places and it has served me well on several occasions. However, despite the fact that it will fit, I actually consider that the TOPS takes up too much space in a tobacco tin for its role and importance, especially since most of the bulk is in the handle.

A smaller version is the CountyComm SERE pocket saw. This is available with a black or orange handle and a red blade in either case. This tool is basically a junior hacksaw blade that folds into a handle. At less than 3" when folded it takes up far less room than the TOPS and is even viable in an Altoids tin.

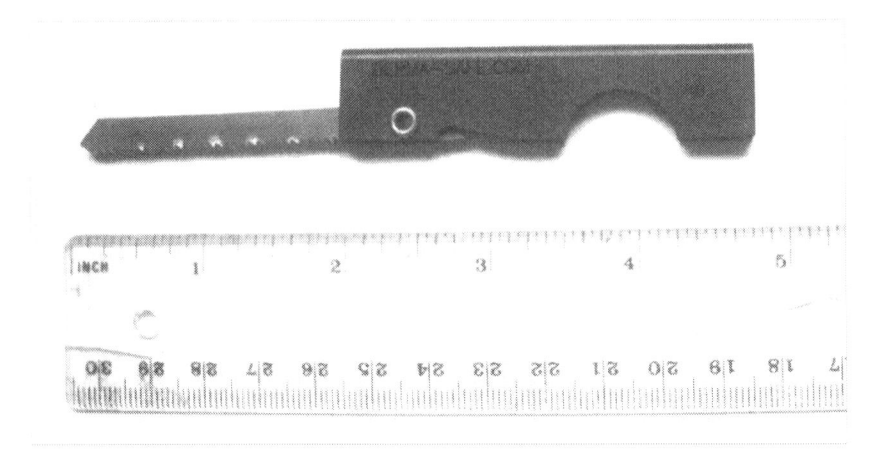

The fine toothed blade works well on soft metals or plastic and will cut wood provided it is neither excessively hard nor thick, but does need regular cleaning to remove the dust from the teeth.

Survival Card saws

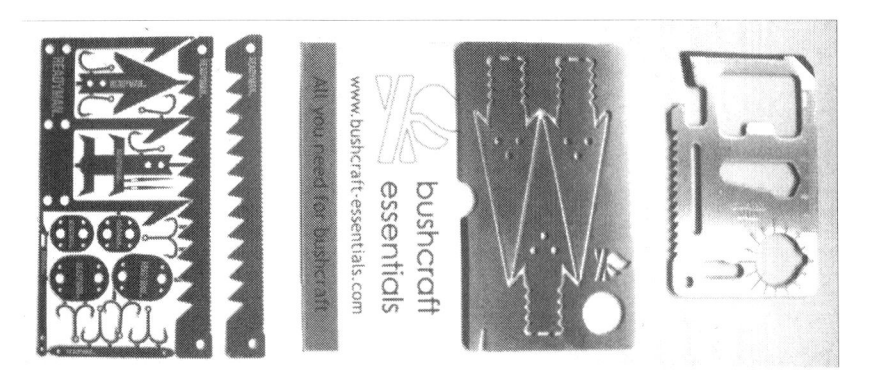

Credit card sized survival tools have quite a fan base in the Prepping movement but they have been around in various forms for many years. Back in the 1980s, Survival Aids sold one that was the original model for many of the cheap, one-piece, multi-tool cards that are available today. Unfortunately not all of the modern examples match the quality of their predecessor and that is particularly true in regards to the saw.

The saw on the SA card was relatively short but had sharp-tipped off-set teeth that cut well on wood or bone. None of the current models I have tried come close in terms of effectiveness and some are so blunt they seem to be there only for appearance sake. The same has to be said of the one on the Bushcraft Essentials card, which has a cutting edge that sharpens well, a wire stripper that is OK, and 3 heavy duty arrow heads. Why they ruin that, on a quite expensive piece of kit, with such a useless saw I don't know; perhaps they just never tried it.

A lesser known card is available from US firm Readyman but currently on sale in the UK at £5.95 from http://www.heinnie.com. This is a card of break-out tools one of which is a dual-edged wood and metal saw.

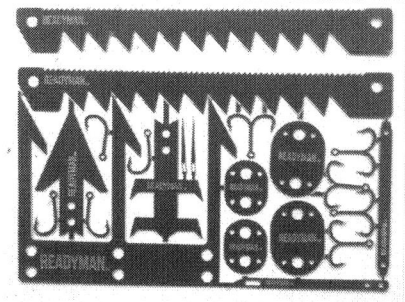

I carried out some extensive testing of the features of these cards, with varying results. The card is about half as thick as most survival cards, or indeed a regular credit card, partly in order to minimise weight and partly to meet the specifications needed by some of the tools e.g. fish hooks and needles. That imposes the need for some care in handling and use but if done properly the saw in particular works well.

While attached to the other items on the card, the hacksaw edge faces outwards and is braced by the card structure. I tested this by cutting through several types of unhardened metal e.g. a window frame and a hasp and staple on which a padlock was securing a gate and also a metal can and it worked effectively.

I then detached the saw and headed to my local woods. Once separated from the other tools the thin blade needs to be put under tension so that it is supported before doing any heavy duty work, rather like a wire saw.

For that I created a miniature bow saw handle into the ends of which I carefully used the saw to cut a couple of slots and then fixed the blade into these using 2 small pegs I carved from a twig. With those in place I tried the saw on several different sized pieces of both hard and soft wood and again it worked well.

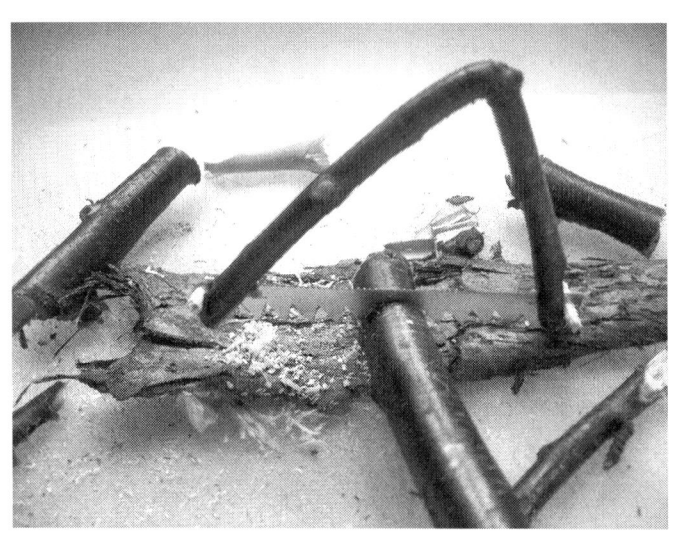

After the saw is detached from the card it takes up very little room in a pocket kit so, providing you have worked out in advance how to use it effectively, it is a good addition. Do bear in mind though, that the temper of the blade is not suited to being used as a striker for ferro rods, which is one function of the next item in this list.

Hacksaw blades

Hacksaw blades are included in military and other PSKs to

serve several roles. As noted above they are often provided as a striker for ferro rods, they can also function as an escape and evasion tool or as a less efficient but still useful general purpose saw. The three above are – top to bottom - from a forces issue kit, a BCB firesteel, and a non-commercial home-built kit.

Their advantage is that they take up minimum space for an important piece of multi-role equipment. Their main disadvantage is that those in many kits are relatively small and difficult to handle. That, however, can be overcome by improvising a grip for them in the same way as you would for a small simple cutting blade.

In the case of the one in this picture, the saw blade also serves yet another role; I have sharpened the end of the blade to provide another cutting tool without taking up any additional space or adding any extra weight to the kit.

In fact the temper of most hacksaw blades makes them eminently suitable for modifying in this way and there are examples where the process has been taken further, to transform the tip and back of the blade into an effective knife while retaining the saw edge to create an even more versatile part of the PSK.

In all, a saw is an adaptable and space-worthy resource for inclusion in your PSK. From the choices available, it need not take up a great deal of space nor add much in the way of weight but can add practical capability. It is an item that is difficult to improvise and for which few other things can act as efficient substitutes. Wherever and for whatever you expect that you might have to use your kit this is a tool to which you should give serious consideration.

Cordage

Cordage is perhaps one of the less essential things to include in an urban PSK because of the amount and variety of potential sources available even after a disaster. Clothes lines, curtain pulls, electrical wiring from wrecked buildings or vehicles, and many other ropes or strings will fall to hand. Even in the city, however, some may be useful in your kit for urgent medical uses such as applying a tourniquet or securing an improvised wound dressing.

In many wilderness areas it is often possible to find natural plant materials that can be used to make cordage, but processing them sometimes takes a considerable amount of time and work, when you might have other urgent things to do, so a good supply is indispensable.

Even in its normal form your urban or country clothing may provide various types of cord but you can improve on that by replacing the provided laces and ties with stronger and more versatile materials such as multi-strand nylon – either genuine parachute cord or one of the similar products now available. That will reduce, if not replace, the need for much within a tin or pouch.

Or paracord can simply be carried rolled in a hank or used as part of the structure or covering of many parts of your PSK.

It is available in a wide range of colours, so finding some that will match what you wear should not be difficult.

For anyone who doesn't know, paracord has an outer sheath of woven nylon and several inner strands – usually 5 or 7 – of thinner nylon thread. Although thin these are still very strong and can serve a wide range of uses from sewing to lashing parts of tools or shelters together. Each end of the cord is usually sealed by being melted but if you clip off or break the ends then the inner cords can be pulled out – individually if you are very careful – leaving the rest intact until needed.

A new variation, called FireCord, even has an additional inner thread – usually red in colour – made from a highly flammable material for use as tinder.

But despite its popularity, strength and versatility, paracord is far from the only form of cordage available.

Thinner cords

For inclusion in tins, pouches or other containers you can choose from any of several types of line.

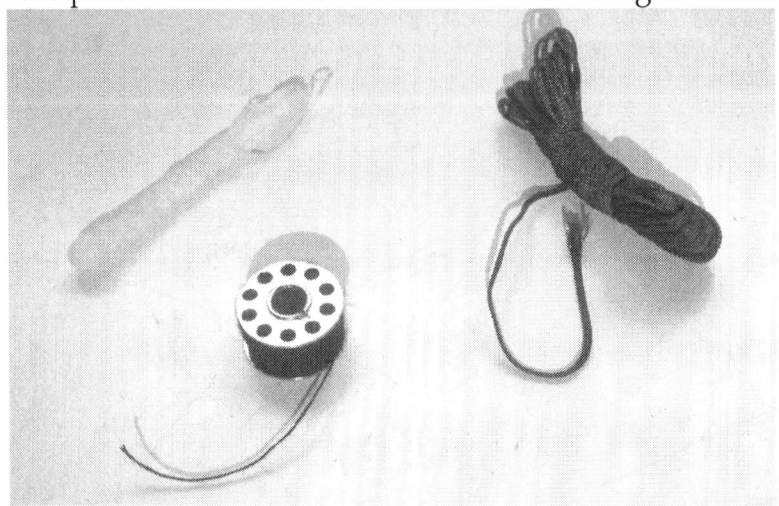

In the picture below I have included – left to right – dental floss, Kevlar cord, and some basic nylon cord.

Dental floss is cheap, easily available, compact and strong. There is 10m length in that small bail. It is usually white and some types have a mint scented/flavoured coating, so might not meet tactical requirements for those for whom that is a consideration, but otherwise it works well for many of the roles in which you might need cordage.

Kevlar is relatively expensive, available from specialist suppliers, even more compact than dental floss – the reel shown holds 20m and costs around £6 - but doesn't stretch and is highly resistant to extreme temperatures, UV, and abrasion. It can be used for clothing and equipment repairs, tool bindings, bow strings, snares, trip lines, and much more. In my opinion, it is worth the cost and space to include a small reel in your kit.

But if neither dental floss nor Kevlar appeals, then thin nylon cord is available in a range of colours from most DIY and garden centres and will meet most of your needs.

Jute string

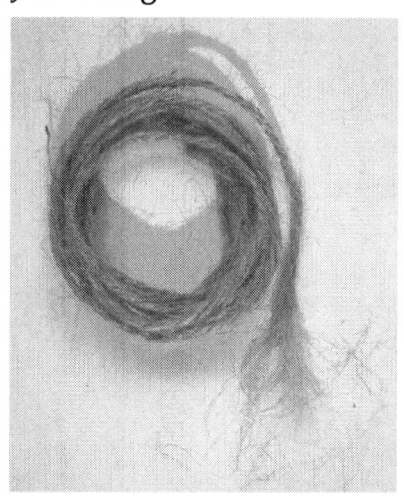

If you can afford the space in your kit or pocket for some 'ordinary' string then you might want to give it to a hank of Jute. Not only is this good general purpose string but if you break it down into a mass of the individual fibres it makes excellent tinder that will light easily from a spark or ember.

Using other items from your kit as cordage
Other items in your PSK, such as brass or steel wire, or

fishing line, can also be used as cordage. However, you do need to consider your priorities and whether they will be best suited to these purposes or the other reasons for which you have included them. This is true of many items within a PSK e.g. do you keep an alcohol swab for cleansing wounds or use it as an easily lit form of tinder; do you adapt safety pins for fishing hooks or save them for repairing clothing?

It is an excellent move to have widely versatile resources within a small set of equipment but you do then face the dilemma of deciding on which potential use should be given priority. Some might be recoverable and having served for one thing will later be able to be put to another, but others will be totally consumed by a single usage. If you are freezing and the alcohol swab is your best chance of starting a fire then the choice is easy, but beware of not including some Kevlar cord because you have brass wire or fishing line when there is the chance that the wire or line might be set out to catch food just when you need cordage for something else.

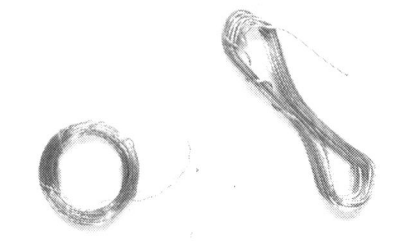

I suppose that since the sub-title of this book is how to use the items in your PSK effectively, I should now write about rigging differing lines and tying various knots but there is so much already out there in print about that, from scout manuals onwards, that I'll assume it is something you already know or can easily research. If I'm wrong about that, email me and I'll write a book just on knots and lines!

Fire starters

A piezo ignited butane lighter, carried close to the body in cold weather, is an easy and reliable fire starter. I choose piezo because the 'flint' (actually a composite sparker material) in lighters that use them can break down after a year or so in storage and fail to spark. The fuel will still be good if you can light it by other means but that rather defeats the purpose of carrying the lighter. I choose butane because petrol in most lighters evaporates after just a few days, whereas gas will be good for years and how much you have left is visible if you buy the right type.

When the lighter is empty of fuel, keep the body to use as a fishing float (1).

A mini lighter will often fit in a kit when full size lighters take too much space. Clipper lighters use butane as fuel but have a flint sparker, though at least some models do have one useful feature; the whole sparker unit can be lifted out and the unit used to make sparks for igniting tinder rather than the fuel in the lighter. I still prefer the piezo style but Clippers do deserve a mention because of that since they can serve the purposes of both lighter and ferro rod. If you choose one of these, carry spare flints and check them regularly to ensure they are still serviceable.

Matches still have their place, provided you keep them and their striker surface dry. Strike anywhere types avoid the problem of a wet or worn striker board; lifeboat matches are waterproof, wind resistant and long burning. They both give you an immediate source of flame but are single use and relatively bulky for the number of strikes you will get compared to the same bulk of a butane lighter.

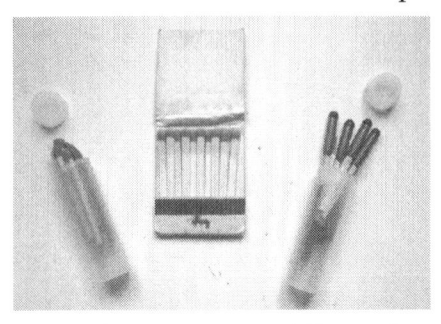

Avoid the 'wind and waterproof' matches that are often available at a very low price. Proper lifeboat matches have a brown head with a black tip and a varnished appearance. The counterfeits have an all red head with a matt finish. Some reviews have said they are OK, others that only some of a batch would light and yet others – including my own experience on 2 occasions – that none of the matches would strike. For survival you need gear you can rely on and matches that don't work can literally be a killer. On very cold days when you have problems making your lighter work and you are out of dry initial tinder a real lifeboat match provides a welcome backup.

Ferrocerium rods are the darling of the Bushcraft crowd. Made from a combination of up to 20 metals with differing properties, some are simply spark rods while others can be carefully scraped to provide a small pile of highly flammable material that you can then ignite using sparks produced by scraping the rod more forcefully. The combination of metals included also controls the temperature of the sparks and fire produced. Very hot sparks and scrapings can ignite tinder that would fail from a less efficient rod.

These rods are one step up from the traditional lump of rock flint and a piece of iron or steel that was used for millennia. They share the flint and steel's requirement for some form of easily ignited tinder that will either produce a glowing ember or a flame. This initial tinder is then used to ignite a larger pile of coarser tinder, which in turn sets fire to kindling and that to fuel. Ferro rods are available in varying sizes from that of a match to hand length and finger thickness.

Some are just a rod, some have a handle and a dedicated striker. The combination of a compatible rod and striker is important for efficient production of sparks.

The main advantages of ferro rods are: they're waterproof, light weight, fairly robust, and can potentially start many fires from even a small one. The main disadvantages are the need for dry, easily ignited tinder to turn sparks into flame and the fact that with most you need 2 serviceable hands, one to hold the rod and the other to wield the striker. Depending on where you are and the weather, finding natural tinder that will work can be difficult, so it is always a good idea to carry some form of initial tinder if you carry a ferro rod.

Do be aware that ferro rods usually come with an air and water proof coating that reduces and delays the deterioration of the rod. Eventually most will start to break down and crumble, though how long they will last in storage depends on the combination of metals used. Before trying to strike sparks with most rods you must scrape off the coating from the area you are going to use, then make a few initial strikes before you start to get good sparks. If you later use a different side of the rod, repeat the preparation process. Having scraped off the coating the metal will now be exposed to air and water so check it more frequently to ensure it is still good and replace the rod with a new one when necessary.

When striking the rod, keep the tip close to the tinder and brace it firmly. Scrape the striker down as much of the length of the rod as possible, to generate the maximum number and brightness of sparks directly into the tinder. If the first strike doesn't cause ignition, repeat it until it does. If you don't get a result, either your tinder isn't dry enough or you're doing something wrong!

Lighters basically work in the same way – creating a spark that ignites fuel to give flame - but single handed and with an integral fuel source that will give a maintainable and easily repeated light. Because of their good features I always include a ferro rod in a PSK, together with some suitable initial tinder, but it is as a second choice firestarter. However, having said it is second choice, rather than retaining it for emergency use only when everything else has failed, my tactic is to use it whenever conditions are favourable and I have suitable tinder and dry kindling and fuel, so as to reserve my preferred lighter and lifeboat matches for more severe conditions or when I am cold, hungry and exhausted and really want a fire as quickly and easily as possible.

Magnesium block fire starters will be familiar to lots of outdoors enthusiasts, Preppers, Survivalists and military personnel, or at least they will know of and have handled them. Being familiar with them, as in having used them, especially having used them successfully, might be a truthful claim of far fewer.

The fact is that there are good examples of these fire starters and some very poor ones. The good ones have a high percentage of magnesium in the alloy of the block, a compatible striker that eases building a pile of shavings and which with a good quality rod produces plenty of large, hot sparks.

The blocks from The Friendly Swede definitely fit in that category whereas some of the cheaper ones from the Far East are almost unusable and poor experiences with them, or lack of knowledge or skill with even good ones can put off many users.

Basically the system is much like any of the others that relies on a spark maker and form of tinder to turn those sparks into flame, which can then be used to ignite increasingly bigger pieces of fuel until you have a fire. The magnesium block is simply a reservoir of tinder. Like most things, Magnesium blocks as tinder have pros and cons:

For:
- The block is compact. A relatively small block will provide enough tinder to give the initial flame for many fires
- The block is waterproof, even without any other packaging
- The block is robust. Unlike a poly bag of cotton wool

or jute it won't become torn and scatter your valuable tinder
- The block is complete i.e. the spark rod is usually attached to it so that you don't end up with tinder but no way to ignite it
- The magnesium shavings burn very hot and can ignite even slightly damp larger tinder

Against:
- Before starting you have to scrape the block in order to remove the coating and then shave off enough magnesium to catch a spark and make a flare
- The magnesium filings are very light and can easily blow away in the wind or wash away in the rain if you do not shield them properly
- The light shavings are easily disturbed and can be scattered if you catch them or create a wind while striking the sparker rod
- You need hot sparks to ignite magnesium tinder, so a compatible ferro rod and striker to go with the block or powder is essential.
- The scrapings burn very fast so you must be ready with a larger quantity of other light materials to catch the flame and build on it
- Knowing the right size of scrapings to create and how much you need depending on what other type of tinder and kindling you have is definitely a knack you need to learn and practise

In a Friendly Swede kit I have tested and reviewed you get: 1 magnesium block with attached flint rod; 1 Scraper/striker washer; 2 approx 4'6" lengths of 350lb breaking strain paracord with 7 interior threads and nylon outer plaited into a lanyard

I really like the striker washer that comes with these kits. For use with the magnesium block and its sparker rod the washer serves efficiently and effectively to: remove the protective coating on block and rod; scrape the block to create a pile of shavings; and strike big hot sparks to ignite them. The serrated edge can also be used to produce excellent fine fuzz curls on kindling sticks, to easily catch the flame from tinder and quickly build the fire.

On my first try with it, the rod and striker worked on the magnesium shavings in just 3 strokes. The tinder pile ignited and then flared bright and hot, to easily set fire to the extra cardboard, bark and shaved wood tinder and kindling I had gathered.

As an alternative to a block you can use a ferro rod and ready prepared magnesium powder. This is available from various sources, in differing sizes of container, or you can make your own.

A Fresnel lens is a flat, usually rectangular but sometimes disc-shaped, plastic magnifying lens that can concentrate light from the sun to produce a high temperature spot which will ignite suitable tinder.

In this regard they work in the same way as any other magnifying lens, such as one from your glasses or a camera or binoculars, but their thin, flat, lightweight, durable format makes them an outstanding choice for inclusion in a PSK. They also serve as a magnifier if you need one for examining a wound or reading fine detail on a map. Their one disadvantage is that they do of course only work for fire starting in sunny conditions, which is often when fire is least essential.

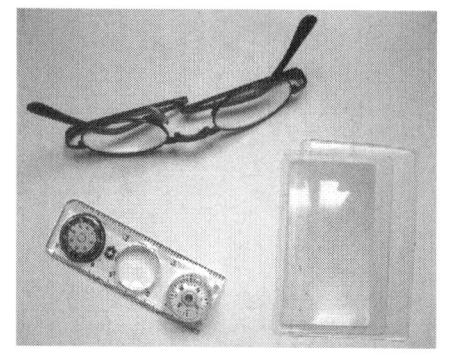

The Fire Piston is an ancient form of fire starter that can still work remarkably well. Many modern forms are now being sold including a few that are small enough to be included in a PSK.

Fire pistons are easy to use; it is simply a case of placing some suitable tinder into the depression in the end of a rod, lubricating a washer around the end of the rod with something like saliva or petroleum jelly and then driving the rod fast and hard into a cylinder in which it forms a close fit. Compressing the air in the cylinder raises its temperature to over 400 degrees and ignites the tinder. If you give the tinder half a second or so to glow and then extract the rod you can then shake out the glowing starter onto suitable dry grass or other tinder and gently blow it into flame.

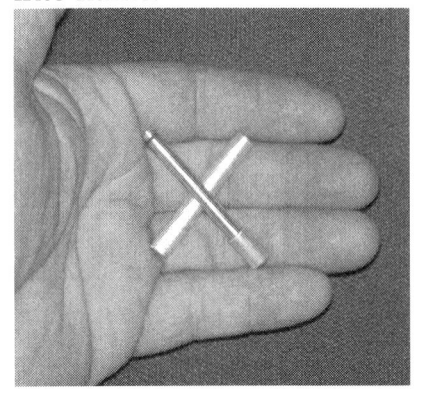

The one shown in this picture is the smallest I have seen. It is the MicroFire from **http://www.minifirepistons. com/MicroFire.htm** It is about 2" long and ¼" in diameter so will easily fit most PSKs. I haven't tried this tiny model, and the ember produced must be very small, but reports from users are good and I have a larger version from the same company that works well.

The only limitation on the use of fire pistons is having suitable tinder. Cotton charcloth works well, as do some natural fungal tinders such as Tinder fungus, Cramp Ball or Chaga. Others, such as seeds from dandelions, cattail or rosebay willowherb will sometimes work but unless they are completely dry often take several tries before they ignite and sometimes won't even then.

Batteries with wire from your PSK can also be used to start fire. Fixing a wire to each terminal of a suitably powerful battery and then touching the ends together will cause sparks that will ignite suitable tinder. Or, if you have some baking foil in your kit you can heat a thin, short, strip of that to fire starting temperature by touching the wires to each end. You can also make fine steel wool glow red hot by putting it across the terminals of batteries but it isn't versatile enough to usually earn a place in a PSK.

But for most of these methods to work, as our ancestors knew only too well, if you are relying on sparks or embers to start a fire then you need to ensure you always have an ample supply of tinder and to keep it dry.

Tinder
If you want to make fire from sparks then you need to carry some initial tinder. There is a wide variety available.

Cotton wool is the simplest, or the lint from a tumble drier will work. These are often enhanced by adding Vaseline to improve waterproofing and extend the burning time.

This combination also has many medical applications of course. If you store the Vaseline separately then you can use the cotton wool to pack out your kit to prevent rattling.

A Tampon is an even more compact and versatile form and I highly recommend including at least 2 in your PSK. Apart from tinder they serve as a wound dressing, plugs for penetrating wounds, water filter, wick for an improvised oil lamp, fletching on darts or arrows, and many other things.

Jute string makes good tinder and can now be had treated or coated with wax or other chemicals for the same benefits as adding Vaseline to cotton wool.

There are many other similar cordage based tinders available, often with fancy names such as 'TinderQuik' or 'Baddest Bee Fire Fuses'. You can tease out one part to easily take a spark and leave the rest compacted for longer burning time. They work well but can be expensive compared to some other tinder.

If you want to make more charcloth, you can either heat cotton fabric in an Altoids or tobacco tin or with it wrapped in baking foil.

Packets or tubes of magnesium filings are available if you don't want to carry a block, as are various other chemical fire starters.

An alcohol pad from your first aid items will light from a spark and burn well for up to a minute. Or, if you carry potassium permanganate as a water purifier and first aid item, and if you have access to the anti-freeze from a vehicle engine, you can make a small pile of powder under your main tinder and kindling, add a similar amount of radiator fluid, and stand back. The reaction sometimes takes a few seconds to build up but then produces an intense flame and acrid smoke. However, one limitation on this is that the reaction may not occur unless the ambient temperature is over 70 degrees Fahrenheit, in which case you won't need fire for warmth though you might want it for signalling, cooking, or boiling water.

Propellant powder from cartridges gives soldiers and shooters a reliable, easily ignited and fast burning supply of tinder.

Removing the bullet or shot and wad from a cartridge will give access to enough powder to provide an initial flame for several fires. Or, while you have access to an ample supply of cartridges, you could empty some powder into a small bag or tube and keep it in your PSK specifically for this purpose.

You can light the powder with a spark from a ferro rod or an ember from a fire piston, or a match or lighter. If you don't have any other sparker, you can position the cartridge case from which you took the powder so that the mouth is close to the pile of powder, place the point of a nail or similar on the primer, then give it a sharp whack with a rock or lump of wood. The flash from the primer will ignite the powder and away you go.

A small piece of a hexamine fuel block can be crumbled to light from a spark and then whole or part blocks added for a longer lasting flame.

Some similar fuel blocks or fire lighters are on sale in supermarkets from the likes of Zip and these have individual wrapping of a material that contains the block if it is crushed, aids water-resistance, and will light from a spark to then ignite the block. Be aware that unlike Hexamine these blocks are said to be safe to burn in an enclosed space but they do produce mucky black smoke.

Hexamine is proven to store for a long time but some of the newer fuel blocks such as WetFire need to be kept with their packaging intact or chemicals evaporate and they will no longer light.

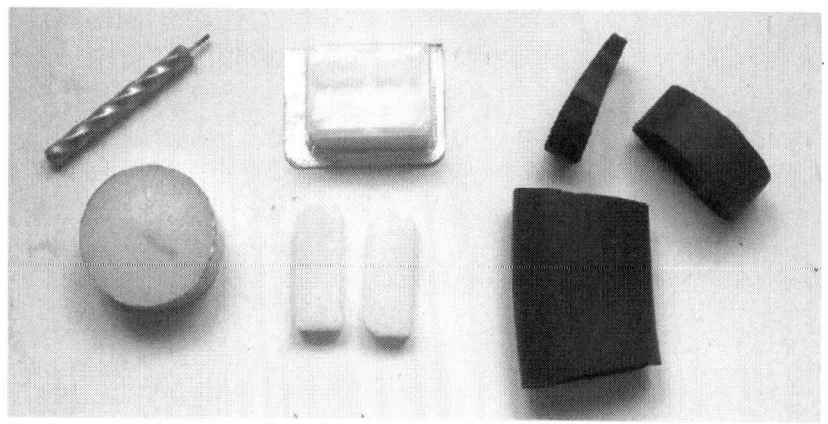

Candles aren't tinder in themselves but are a 'tinder-extender' popular in PSKs. Night or 'tea' lights are often used in this role, but slices from long-life stearine candles also work well. Birthday cake candles offer a compact alternative and trick ones that won't blow out can be useful in gusty winds.

Ranger bands are nothing more than strips of rubber, often cut from inner tubes. Large inner tubes from mountain bikes provide bands of a good size for sealing PSK tins and the rubber is also a waterproof and durable source of flame when lit. It won't usually light from a spark or ember so you would have to use those to start a small flame but that will then ignite the rubber for a longer lasting starter to set your kindling burning.

I will guess that from the amount of detail above and the fact that using the various options effectively has its own chapter, you will realise how much importance I give to fire starting materials in your PSK.

Despite the threats of giving away your position, there are times when fire to warm you or purify water or cook food that would be dangerous raw is absolutely essential for survival. I recommend having at least 3 fire starter options in your kit – most often a lighter, matches and a ferro rod plus tinder – if space possibly permits. If it doesn't then carry a lighter separately, or stuff part of your clothing with suitable tinder or whatever but don't neglect fire making resources.

Water

After shelter and warmth, the next priority in your survival needs is clean water.

Depending on the environment you might be able to collect water in liquid form from a stream or water soaked ground or rain, or you might have to soak up dew or steam if the available ground water is salty or heavily contaminated.

For collecting water you will want a pan or bag. A length of plastic tubing is sometimes useful for reaching into otherwise inaccessible collection points. Your kit container or a folded length of foil could be used as the pan, the bag could be a non-lubricated condom, Ziploc, breast milk, or Pour & Store bag. If you use a condom, support the filled container in a pocket lining or sock to protect it.

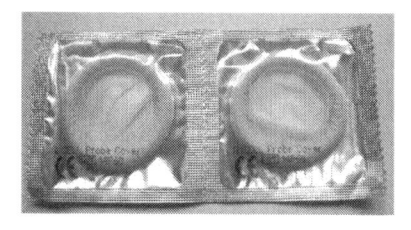

The tube could initially be used as a waterproof container for other kit, perhaps within a paracord wristband, or one of your medical items for opening an airway or tying a tourniquet, or a catapult power band for hunting.

For collecting dew or condensed steam, military aircraft survival kits contain a compressed sponge but you can use any piece of absorbent cloth for the same purpose and then squeeze or wring it out into your container. A cotton bandana is excellent for the purpose. (1)

Purifying water often requires 2 steps: first filtration to

remove as much suspended matter as possible and then disinfection to kill any remaining bugs. In some environments there might also be chemical or other contaminants and if this is a threat then more thorough filtration using several layers of increasing fineness and including layers of charcoal are needed.

Depending on the size of your PSK, you could carry a cloth filter, such as a Millbank bag, or paper filters such as those used for coffee. Alternatively you could improvise using bandages or wound pads, or a tampon, or even parts of your clothing such as pocket pouches, in a container improvised from tree bark, together with layers of sand, grit, moss or grass, and charcoal. Arrange your layers so that the further down the water goes the finer the filter material becomes. You can put layers of charcoal scraped from the wood of your fire between any of the other layers.

After the water is filtered, chemical sterilisers, such as chlorine or iodine tablets will work more effectively. You can carry a supply of chlorine tablets sealed in strips or you could pack more in a tiny Ziploc bag but iodine needs to be in a sealed glass bottle. In either case, take note of the expiry date. After this the tablets won't directly become dangerous to use but they will gradually lose effectiveness so you might think you are treating your water but not actually be killing any bugs it contains.

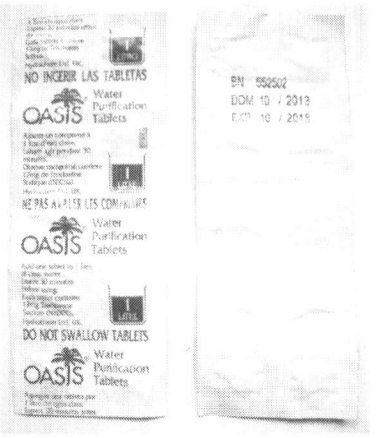

Most people prefer the taste of the chlorine to iodine

and iodine is not recommended for people with thyroid problems but it does serve as a protective agent to flood the thyroid if there is any danger from fallout containing radioactive iodine. Because of the taste, iodine tablets often come with, or have available as a separate item, additional pills or powder to neutralise them after they have been given time to sterilise the water. Other sources of Vitamin C will also serve for that purpose.

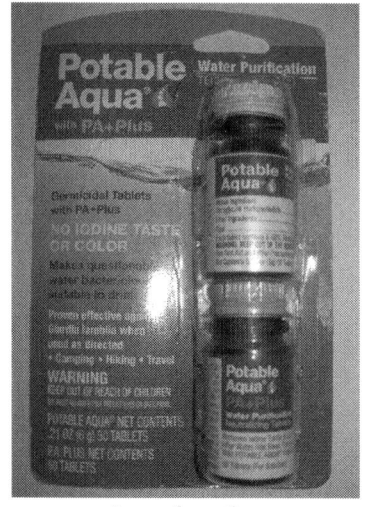

Alternatively, you could carry a small bottle of thin unscented bleach, which is cheaper but bulkier and less convenient for the same amount of water as the tablets.

Potassium Permanganate was a popular choice for water purification at one time, as it can also be used in varying strengths for disinfecting wounds and equipment to be used for medical purposes, or for colouring snow as emergency signals to potential rescuers, or with other chemicals for starting fires. It has fallen from favour because you do need experience in judging the correct depth of colour that represents correct strength for various purposes and if you get it too weak it isn't effective, if too strong it can cause problems. A pale pink colour is right for drinking water. Chlorine tablets are simpler as you just use 1 per litre of water and leave for 30 minutes – or longer if the water is still cloudy after being filtered – before use.

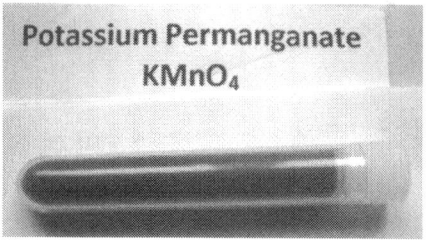

One piece of gear you could have in your PSK is a

73

purification straw. These perform the roles of collection, filtration and purification in a convenient and easy to use form.

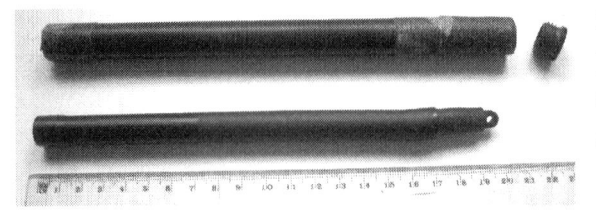

They are not generally expensive and are lightweight and quite thin but might be too long for your on-the-body kit unless you have or add a narrow pocket of sufficient length.

Another product that is popular at the moment is the mini water filter from Sawyer. It works very well and certainly doesn't take up a massive amount of room in a survival bag but, like most straws, it is slightly too big for most small PSKs.

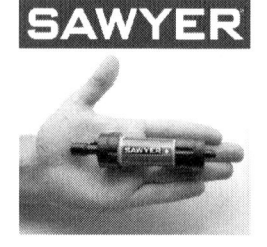

Your kit could also hold a length of aluminium foil, such as heavy duty baking foil, which you can form into a pan in which to boil water. If your PSK container is a small tin then you could use that but it will almost certainly hold much less than a pan made from a reasonable size piece of foil. Raise the water temperature to a rolling boil and keep it there for at least 5 minutes to properly sterilise it at sea level. Increase the boiling time by 1 minute per thousand feet of elevation because the boiling point of water drops as air pressure does.

With these items in your kit, and the use of a bit of initiative, you should be able to collect water and avoid any health problems from it.

Food

You aren't going to fit anything much in the way of ready-to-eat food supplies into any PSK but some people do include a couple of pieces of barley sugar or Kendal mint cake to provide a quick sugar rush when it is really needed. Otherwise the main components tend to be condiments, particularly salt, pepper, spices, or a stock cube, or a couple of individual sachets of coffee. In addition to adding flavour, the salt and stock cubes are particularly valuable for replacing salt lost in sweat during heavy activity.

Beyond these basics, most of what you might pack will be things to provide food by hunting, fishing or foraging.

Wire for making snares or a trap is a common food gathering feature of PSKs.

This is most often brass wire but some people prefer steel. Some users keep it as simple wire until needed, others will carry it ready made into snares and unwind one if they need the wire for other things. Take your pick depending on your most likely uses of the wire and the law where you will carry the kit.

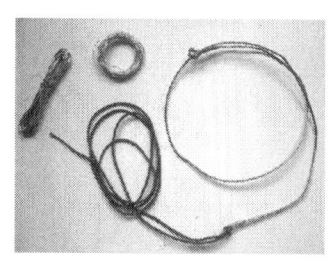

A single thickness of steel wire is sufficient for rabbit sized game but brass wire is normally wound with 6 or 8 strands.

To make your brass snare: cut a stick of about finger thickness and shave it smooth. Fix a pole upright and clear at the top. Wrap one end of the wire around the stick 3 or 4 times and then around the free part of the wire to secure it. Hold the stick about 18" away from the pole. Loop the wire around the pole, and then back around the stick. Repeat that 3 or 4 times. Secure the loose end of the wire by wrapping it tightly around both sides of the loop just in front of the stick, pulling them tightly together. Brace the pole and pull back on the stick to pull the wire tight. Now keeping the wire taut, twist the stick around and around until the wire is wound into a single strand all the way along. Slip the wire off the pole and give that end a few extra twists to narrow the open loop. Slip the wire off the stick and thread the pole end through the round hole that had the stick through it. Attach some cordage to the loop that was at the pole end. You now have a snare that should pull closed smoothly when your prey is caught in it.

For neck or leg snares for larger game follow the same procedure with steel wire or as above but with more strands with brass wire.

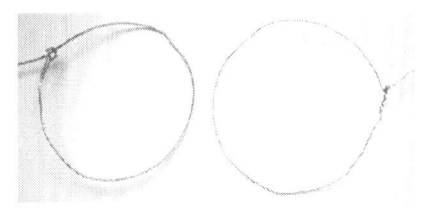

Making a single strand snare of either steel wire or brass wire for smaller game, such as squirrels or birds, is even easier. Simply wrap one end of the wire around a stick a couple of times and then around the wire in front of the stick to form a loop. Remove the stick and pass the other end of the wire through the loop. Form another loop on the free end to attach cordage for securing the snare to a stake or pull-up.

For a rabbit the neck loop wants to be about a clenched fist wide and set 4 fingers high off the ground. For other game and leg snares adjust the size of the loop and the height it is set according to the size of the prey and type of trap.

After you have made your snares try to remove any of your own scent from the wire or cord by rubbing it with grass or the fur or dung of the prey and then keep it in a bag or wrapped in leaves. Before handling again rub your hands with dirt or leaves.

Arrow heads in the form of survival cards that include

one or more points attached by a couple of small tabs so that they can be easily broken out are a relatively recent arrival on the survival scene.

These are flat, well pointed and barbed but not usually sharpened on the edges. The cards are the same thickness and size as a credit card, sometimes thinner and smaller, so they will fit easily into or on the outside of most PSK containers.

You could also break off one or more of the arrowheads for inclusion in kits but the cards sometimes have additional features, such as saw, knife or even axe edges, spanners, wire cutters/nail pullers, and others, so the choice is yours depending on whether you want/need those extra functions. As previously mentioned for survival cards re their saw edges, do a thorough evaluation of the efficiency of these extra tools before committing to including one because of them; not all perform very well.

It is unlikely that you would go to the effort of making a bow for hunting or defence unless you expected your survival situation to become long term or seriously aggressive, so whether to give space and weight allowance to arrow heads is a consideration.

If you believe a bow is needed, then Kevlar cord would be a sound choice for cordage, because it makes a decent bow string due to its strength and resistance to stretching. If you prefer to stick with paracord then 4 or more of the inner strands twisted into a single line will also serve in this role, as will heavy duty fishing line.

Catapult bands and ammo are sometimes included in a PSK if the owner seriously expects to need to hunt or have a simple weapon for self defence at relatively short range.

Some users include flat elastic bands or tubes and will improvise the pocket and ammo; others go for a commercial setup. It is an option, but one I tend to leave for caches or bag based kits due to the space needed, although if I wanted one I might consider building it into a paracord belt kit since the materials are so flexible.

Fishing kit is a far more conventional inclusion in a PSK. Some kits feature almost everything except a rod and reel but for survival fishing all you really need is hooks, line and sinkers. You can usually find live bait but an artificial fly, maggots or worm don't take up much space or add much weight so you might consider them.

The thing with survival fishing is that in the early days you rarely have time to sit on a river or lake bank watching a float in the water and in many situations nor do you have the luxury of doing so in sight of people who might come to hurt you or steal whatever you have caught. That means that the normal method of fishing is to set night lines.

These consist of a fairly heavy line across a river/stream or from a bank or tree down into the water, from which run thinner weighted lines carrying baited hooks to various levels from the surface to the bed. With these you have the chance of catching fish of various species, some of which will be bottom feeders, some mid stream and some surface predators. Live bait might be taken at any level but if you can't find any then your artificial fly might attract fish at the surface or below and the fake maggots or worm at other levels.

If hostile people might spot your position because of the line, then you set it out at last light and retrieve it early in the morning. If your position is more secure then you can leave it in position all day, check it evening and morning, and renew the bait when required.

For your PSK I recommend 25 yards of 20lb or heavier line (you can extend it with inner strands from paracord if needs be) 5 or 6 hooks no larger than #10 and mostly #12 or 14 - preferably already tied to differing lengths of line of from 5 to 10 ft of 5 or 6lb breaking strain, or otherwise with 15yards of that line - 12 BB size sinkers, and maybe 1 or 2 small artificial flies and half a dozen fake maggots. You don't really need floats or swivels or anything else fancy.

The main problem with most commercial survival fishing kits is that the hooks are all too big. Those hooks are fine for sea fishing or big rivers where you get large carp or salmon but not for most fresh water. One of the truisms that you will hear in survival circles is, 'big hooks only catch big fish, little hooks catch little and big fish!' While a catching a big fish is great, you will get far more bites from smaller fish that will not take a big hook. In the long run, the weight of food you land from many small fish will be more than you would get from a few big ones. Besides which there might not be any big fish at all in the stretch of water you are fishing in which case only the small hooks would ever be productive.

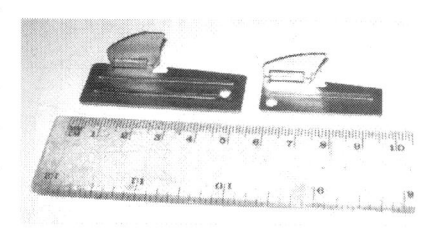

Tin openers are mainly, but not solely, an item for the urban PSK. On the Internet you will see demonstrations of opening a tin by rubbing it on concrete but in reality it is much harder work than it appears and you can end up with your food contaminated by metal and stone filings and dirt. The P-38 or slightly larger P-51 tin openers are widely available for less than a pound. Some users recommend the P-51 as easier to use but I've never had any problems with the P-38. Either way, do yourself a favour and find space for one in your kit.

Aluminium foil is so useful for cooking the things you forage that considering how little space and weight it takes it is worth its place for this purpose as well as its other uses. Some of the plants you find and possibly some of the meat you scavenge will only be safe to eat if you cook them.

You can make the foil into a pan to boil or fry your catch or wrap it around the food to roast it in the embers of the fire other essentials in your PSK will enable you to start.

In areas with strong sunshine it might also be possible to form the foil into a parabolic reflector. That would enable you to use the heat directly for cooking (1).

However, reports of the viability of even purpose built reflectors vary in UK and here in Scotland I might try it but I wouldn't bet on the chances of success!

Navigation

The Button Compass

Button compasses have been around for a long time. In WW2 they actually were concealed in the metal buttons on military – particularly RAF aircrew – uniform. Since then they have become a feature of many pieces of survival equipment as well as being included in most Service and civilian PSKs.

There are basically 2 types, liquid filled and dry pivot. The liquid filling is used to dampen the movement of the compass needle or disk, which can be unsteady and difficult to orient when held in a hand shaking from cold, exertion or stress. Unfortunately, cheaper liquid filled compasses are prone to leaking and the development of bubbles (note: bubbles can also form due to pressure changes from variations in temperature or elevation above sea level).

While they are small the bubbles might not have any noticeable effect but if they get big they can stop the needle/disk from rotating and aligning properly with north. If that happens, you can try piercing the casing with a hot needle or a fine drill bit and draining out the fluid. Some compasses will then act as a viable dry pivot model but others are so unstable they are unusable.

In yet others, the disk actually floats in the fluid instead of resting on a pivot and draining them renders the compass completely inoperable. Many are so cheap that if an attempted repair doesn't work you can afford to discard them and buy a new one but that doesn't help if you are in the middle of nowhere in an emergency and you need to know which way you are going.

That said, a few with appropriately formed casings deliberately include a bubble to allow for pressure variations and on some, such as the one on the Victorinox Traveller set, it is described as a feature for use as a spirit level.

Most button compasses are very simple, disk shaped containers containing the magnetised needle or disk, which might be marked with as little as a couple of luminous dots or a range of letters designating cardinal points. A few - such as the excellent Silva Carabiner 28 (on the left on first picture) - have a base plate, and some newer ones include a rotatable bearing-marked bevel that allows them to be used more like a full scale model.

In most cases the compass is used by balancing it on the palm of the hand, often with the side of the hand held against the abdomen, noting the direction of north and then turning to face the desired direction of travel. The traveller then selects a landmark or reference point on the required bearing and sets off in that direction.

The difficulty comes in the dark or other conditions where you can't see a usable reference point. In that case you have to keep using the compass to ensure you are going in the right direction. To help in that, you can place a marker, such as a piece of tape, on the edge of the compass at the north point before you begin, and then by checking the north pointer is aligned with your marker, that you are still on your chosen bearing.

Your skill in keeping direction using this method definitely improves with practise, but it is good for general direction at best; fine if you know that you are heading for a border or safe zone to the south west, for example, but not the best if you have to navigate between known minefields or avoid falling over a cliff edge on the way.

Whenever possible, I find that it is more accurate to improvise a base plate. I usually carry a small notebook as part of my PSK and in the back of that I have a sheet of waterproof paper marked up for using the compass. Each of my mini kits has a sheet of paper that is similarly marked.

If that isn't available though, you can make a simple version using any scrap piece of plain paper, card, soft (non-ferrous) metal, bark or even a leaf, with markings drawn or scratched onto it. With a modern mini compass with a bevel you then have a miniature of a main compass but even with a simple model, by marking your original north point you have a much more accurate aid to keeping direction.

So the button compass is perhaps far more capable than many people give it credit for, but as with so much of the equipment in PSKs getting best use from it requires some additional techniques and lots of practise.

Shadow compass

If you don't have a compass or it fails, and if the sun is bright enough to cast a shadow, you could use your saw and knife to cut sticks to make a shadow compass. (1)

Simply: if you plant a stick upright on a sunny day it will cast a shadow. Since the sun moves from the east, through the south, to the west (in the northern hemisphere), so the shadow will gradually move the opposite way i.e. towards the east. When you first plant the stick, mark the tip of the shadow with a stone or another stick. Later, after there is a noticeable move in the position of the shadow, mark the new position. Because the sun moves through the south, a line half way between the two shadows away from your main stick will point north.

Maps

Even a low-detail small scale map covering a large area can be useful if you might have a long distance to travel but otherwise more detail will always be helpful. For an urban kit an Ordnance Survey map covering a city area will at least show you the roads, railway lines, canals, rivers, parks and footpaths, contours and some major landmarks but a street map would be even better. You could highlight some particularly important landmarks to make them easier to spot on the map. If the destruction is heavy and widespread then the collapse of buildings and consequent loss of road names and street signs will be confusing but some of the larger monuments and landmark buildings may still be identifiable so that you can at least work out which way you are facing and plan some sort of route towards a safer area.

Remember that route might not be the shortest way home but one that will avoid major hazards or obstacles until you are clear of the worst affected zones and can then turn towards your intended destination. If you know the demographic structure of the city then you should also know which areas are best avoided at any time, let alone when there is chaos in the streets.

Since bridges and tunnels could be damaged or blocked, rivers can be a major obstacle. However, when the World Trade Centre was hit, many people from the area headed towards the waterfront where they found access to ferries and boats of all kinds with owners ready to make multiple journeys to transport survivors across the river. Whether that is an option depends on the nature of the disaster but alternative routes or transport such as that, or along canals and their towpaths, or on foot alongside railway lines should be considerations you are ready to evaluate.

One of the vital features of OS maps is the contour line and spot height system and when destruction of an urban area is on a massive scale these can be as vital for navigation as they are in wilderness areas. They are also important for planning your route if, for example, you are trying to escape or avoid flooding.

To include a map in a PSK, cut it down to the smallest area practical and then either laminate or spray-waterproof it before folding it tightly. If you need a reminder of some of the information on features and symbols or true/magnetic/grid bearing variation then make your own notes on the back of the map before you waterproof it.

You can also get mapping, compass and Satnav apps on smart phones that do not rely on you having a connection to a network. They vary in quality but some are well regarded and are particularly useful if you have to travel beyond the range of any paper maps you have in your kit. If you have a suitable phone then do a search online for apps that are suited to your operating system, search for independent reviews and try some out in your area.

For starters, Locus Map Pro and OrusMaps Offline Maps are well thought of by Android users. Maps.Me and

MotionX have good reports for iPhone. All these are offline so you don't need to have a mobile signal to use them but they do rely on you having battery power for your phone, so they are additions to, rather than replacements for, physical resources.

Pencil and paper

If you have a map then with a couple of sheets of waterproof paper and a pencil with eraser in your kit you can make notes of bearings and distances for various stages of your journey and of important landmarks or potential sources of supply along the way. Not everyone is naturally cool and focussed in an emergency and if you are not one of those then stress and fatigue can lead to forgetfulness and mistakes. Don't be over-confident about this unless you have knowledge born of experience about how you react. Give yourself the best chance by using whatever aids you've got.

If you don't have a map then try to find any vantage point that will give you a view of the area and what has happened within it. From what you can see, decide the direction you need to go and use your pencil and paper to draw a sketch map and notes as above.

Having a pencil with an eraser means that after you have covered one stage of your journey you can delete that information and have space to make another map or notes. If you have to sharpen the pencil keep the shavings, they make excellent tinder.

You can also mark the edges of the paper with either standard measurements in cm/mm or inches or divisions that match differing scales of maps, and to make a template on one side of one sheet to act as a compass baseplate as shown earlier in this chapter.

Signalling

Whistles

There are plenty of whistles to choose from online but most are rubbish! Many kits and other pieces of equipment – such as the firestarter buckles now popular on paracord wristbands – contain whistles and some are better than nothing (others not much better!) as a backup but you shouldn't rely on them as your primary signalling device if you can have something louder with you. What you need is a rescue recommended model that has been tested and rated as having an output of 100decibels or higher. Cheapest if you can find one is a military surplus lifejacket whistle but even good commercial models can be had for a few pounds.

The classic Acme model 636 - Sea and Mountain Rescue whistle is compact and usually available for less than £2 but is approved by the Safety of Life at Sea International Regulations. It is also used by the Mountain Rescue Council and is the Official Ramblers Whistle. The model 558 plastic Thunderer is also a good choice but slightly bulkier than the 636.

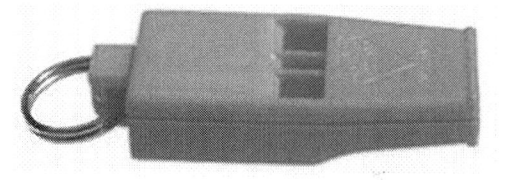

The Adventure Medical Kits Sol Rescue Howler, or its more compact 'Slim' version from the same firm in the USA, works well. It is slightly more expensive than some of the other models but you will still get 2 for less than £5. The whistle from TOPS knives for less than £3 will also meet the need.

The official advice on correct distress use, as given by Mountain Rescue for England and Wales is, "Six good long blasts. Stop for one minute. Repeat. Carry on the whistle blasts until someone reaches you and don't stop because you've heard a reply – rescuers may be using your blasts as a direction finder." The official reply is 3 blasts but some teams don't use that because they have found that the casualty sometimes stops calling if they reply and they then have more difficulty zeroing in on them.

The great advantage of a whistle is that you can carry on using one long after your voice would have given out if you were shouting for help. They are light and compact so there is no reason not to have one in either an urban or wilderness PSK.

If you have access to a vehicle then the horn can be an alternative audible signal, or you might use a pot or any other piece of metal with whatever comes to hand as a hammer to bang it.

In very cold conditions, a plastic whistle is preferable to a metal one because it is less likely to freeze to your lips (1).

Torch

There is more information on models suitable for inclusion in personal kits in the next chapter on Light Sources but let's say here that for signalling some have additional features built in, such as a strobe effect, but for distress purposes brightness and projection are the most important aspects. Some are focussed to give a bright light over a short distance and others are designed to reach out. Some are adjustable to cover both. Bear in mind that greater brightness means less battery life so either spare batteries or a recharging facility, or both, is desirable.

Some users, especially in urban areas, have moved from carrying a torch to relying on a flashlight app on the their phone; that is a good backup or can remove one item from the list of things you carry but it does impose a heavy drain on the phone battery and your phone might be better put to other purposes. However there are reports of instances where even the normal background light of the phone has been used to give rescue parties a location marker to a casualty, so it is worth trying.

In urban areas vehicle lights could be used or any other lamp improvised from a battery, bulb, and a couple of bits of wire and tape from your kit.

Glow sticks

Except in quite open areas, the mini sticks you might include in your kit are not highly visible at long distance but if you have enough then you could use them to try to indicate your position to search aircraft or boats, or in formation in accordance with the international emergency codes.

In closer conditions they are likely to attract the attention of rescuers trying to make their way towards you, even if they don't initially realise where the light is coming from.

Mirror

Mirrors for signalling and communication have been proven in use for millennia. The Romans, Greeks, Egyptians and many other societies all used them. They are still a recommended feature of all official military and commercial vessel survival kits.

The advantage over a torch of course is that they don't need batteries; the disadvantage is that they do need sun or moonlight, so both a torch and mirror are valid items for the kit. They are also useful for checking wounds in places you can't see directly or for admiring your camouflage makeup if you are going all tactical.

Probably the most highly regarded commercial model is the Starflash Ultra, which is used by some military organisations, but its casing makes it rather bulky. There is a more compact Micro version or many others available commercially. There are also polished steel 'dogtag' mirrors available. They are less efficient than larger models but easy to carry. Do beware of the coated plastic 'heliographs' in some commercial PSKs. Many are practically useless so don't rely on one unless you have had it out, removed the protective cover, and actually tested it with someone at a distance.

On the military surplus scene, look for the RAF signal mirror, which is only about 50x50mm/2" square (although there is also a bigger one 100x100mm/4" square), solid steel, has an aiming hole in the centre, instructions on the back and a plastic 'foresight' to help with directing the flash at your target.

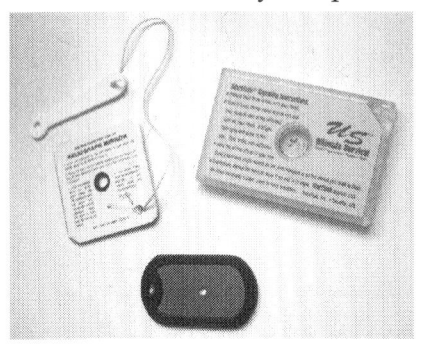

Much cheaper, bigger and simpler, but less often available these days, is the old military mirror, which is a flat rectangular piece of polished steel with a hole in the centre for signalling and another near the edge on one side to use for hanging it for use when shaving, etc.

As an urban alternative, scavenge a wing or rear view mirror, or even a reflector from a headlight from any wrecked vehicle or a makeup compact from a discarded handbag. In the wilderness you could try a polished surface on a survival tin or your baking foil. If you go for baking foil then try to find a solid, flat object to use as a backing, wrap the foil over it and then smooth it as clear of creases as possible. If desperate, people have successfully used knife blades and even one report of attracting help by flashing with the hologram on their credit card. Anything is worth a try but do carry something more credible if practical.

Fire

Of course your PSK should contain several tools for making fire and both the light and smoke can be used for signalling. The important thing is to have the fires well prepared for fast ignition and development of the fire and smoke.

As always, choose an area where it will be safe to have the fire. The recognised distress configuration is 3 fires in a triangle with at least 10m between each fire.

Because you want the tinder to take and the fire to develop quickly, if you have suitable materials build 3 tripods, each containing a platform. On the platform position dry tinder that will ignite quickly from the firestarters within your PSK and thoroughly dry kindling and fuel over that. The platform will raise your tinder off the ground to keep it dry and enhance the air flow to speed the build up of the fire.

Over the fuel, on the outside of the tripod, build a thatch of green vegetation that will protect the fire materials from rain or too much wind and that will burn to provide plenty of smoke.

In urban areas, wreckage can provide the structure for the fire and differing sizes of tyres for the cover. Scavenged fuel from vehicles or other abandoned sources will help to light them quickly.

Be ready to light your signal as soon as you see or hear anyone whose attention you might be able to attract.

Potassium permanganate

When mixed with water this chemical creates a purple dye that imparts a strong stain. On snow or ice, or less durably on sand, it will enable you to create internationally recognised distress signals. You can use the powder directly on snow but you will get better area coverage by mixing it with water and scattering or spraying that.

Alternatively you could use the saw from your kit to cut vegetation to make the signs.

The most basic signals are: a large V which indicates 'need assistance'; or an equally large X which means 'unable to proceed' or 'need medical assistance'. There are many more that can be used to expand on that or you could simply write HELP or SOS in large letters and anyone who spots it should get the message.

Tape

Brightly coloured tape from your kit could also be used for wrapped or dangle markers on trees, etc. (1)

Phone

Getting all modern, if you have a mobile phone and can get a signal then you can of course just try to call for help. Many survivors have found the network totally blocked after a disaster, either with other people trying to call out or their friends and relatives calling in, but if you can't make a voice call you might well be able to send a text or, if you can get online, an email. The response might be a lot slower but it is better than nothing.

Radio

For incoming information on a disaster, there are some truly tiny radios available that might lock onto a useful station and which might be worth space in your PSK. As I write this in December 2015, a local radio station for the north west of England, has been recognised in parliament as a major aid and source of information both to those affected by flooding and from ones phoning into the station's live broadcast asking for help when they didn't know who else to call or couldn't contact them.

For outgoing signals, a wilderness or military kit might feature either a CB or HF radio or a Personal Locator Beacon that will transmit a distress signal that will be detected by satellites. The information from these can then allow triangulation of your position. Depending on the type this could be down to within 100m or even 10m and, increasingly, closer than that.

It might seem that in this section I've gone a little beyond the basics of what you can actually do with items within your PSK but since rescue is often the best way out of a survival situation and your kit might include survival references that will show the various emergency signals but not all of the ways to create them, I'm happy to stretch it a bit.

Light sources

Torches

We are now blessed with a wide range of extremely bright and compact torches with a variety of features. The development of LEDs has greatly lengthened either the battery life or the brightness that can be obtained for the same battery life that was available using standard bulbs.

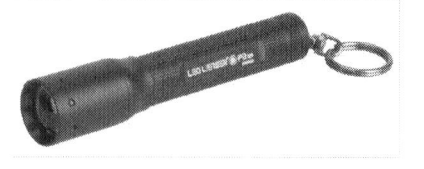

New batteries have aided in this development but whether to choose a torch that uses one of the new cells or a more traditional one, such as AAA or AA, deserves some consideration. For a wilderness kit for a civilian a new type battery such as the CR123A with whatever spares you can fit in is a logical choice, but for a soldier or an urban kit, where there is more chance of resupply if your light uses a traditional battery, then one of those makes more sense.

Of course if the torch that makes sense for you is one of the tiny 'key ring' range e.g. a Photon Microlight or a Streamlight, that takes button cells then you have to go with those tiny power sources.

Then again, there are tiny wind-up key ring lights with 2 or 3 LEDs that use a built-in miniature dynamo to charge them. They aren't nearly as bright as many of the battery powered torches but they do have the advantage of longevity in use, though you should check them regularly after a couple of years because they do deteriorate in storage if not used.

If you have room, you might even decide that a light source is so important for you that you should incorporate both a pen-sized torch and a key ring light as a backup.

Another consideration should be how bright you want the torch to be. The obvious answer is, 'as bright as I can have' but that isn't always the best option. A high lumen rating is ideal for signalling or if you need to search the ground ahead at a distance but in many cases you don't need that much power, in order to read a map or prevent you falling over rubble or foliage for example, and brighter light might attract unwanted attention.

Less light output also often means greater battery life. Some models do give you the option of several output levels and even flashing or automatic signalling modes but check on how these are accessed because with some you have to work through different settings starting at the higher levels.

Soldiers often tape over much of the lens of issue torches to reduce the output to just enough for what they usually need, you might decide to do the same.

Another choice is the format. Do you want a hand torch, perhaps with features that extend it's usefulness as a defensive weapon, or a head torch that lets you operate hands-free, or something that with a simple headband will work in both ways?

Which to choose? There are some names that have become known as reliable options, though their models are not always cheap. Take a look at Fenix, LED Lenser, Petzl, Maglight, Proton and Streamlight for starters, though there are very cheap models available from many outlets that might satisfy your requirements just as well.

Glow sticks

In some, and especially the very small packages, mini glow sticks are chosen as the light source. They have the advantages of being operable in almost all weather, temperature and pressure conditions, are relatively long storage-life, compact and light weight. They are not as bright as even the smallest of most torches and are one-time activation but even so, they do have many good uses.

These were originally intended for night fishing, and can serve that purpose as either a dip indicator or an attractant, if appropriate in your survival situation, but more likely they will be of use as a light or marker.

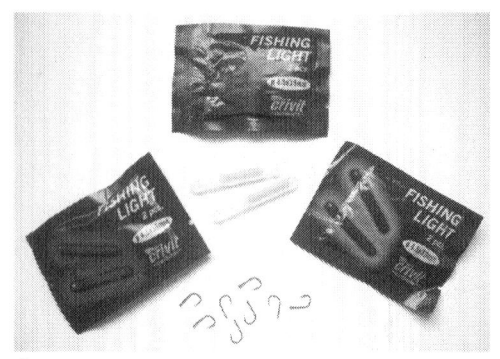

When illuminated the sticks give off their light in all directions and this can be useful, wasteful, or a potential hazard. For use as a light, place them in front of a reflective surface e.g. heliograph (signal mirror), polished tin surface, or aluminium foil, to give you best use of the light. Your sticks are single use and maximum light time is limited, so plan and organise the tasks for which you will need them so that you can do as many as possible during their most effective output period.

Glow times of these tiny sticks will vary with the type of rod and manufacturer but the average seems to be about 4 hours useful light and another 2-4 hours as a marker.

Various colours are available and you should choose in accordance with your intended purpose. From brightest downwards the colour scale is: green, yellow, orange, purple, white (usually tinged with blue), blue, pink, red. Yellow is easiest to read by but if you are using them with a map remember that some colours can hide the features of similar colour on the paper. Red will protect your night vision.

For other uses: if you are trapped in very dark conditions due to a building collapse or a breakdown on the underground or power failure elsewhere with no natural light and emergency lighting fails, then a glow stick can be a welcome aid to morale as well as a useful resource for movement or self-rescue actions.

When moving as a group in very dark conditions, a small glow rod attached to the back of each person – except for the rear most – can make it easier for those in line to follow their leader. You could maintain physical contact or use a string but the extra distance that the light gives can aid safety, giving the next in line time to react if the leader stumbles over an obstacle. Just remember that the glow stick is there and, if you turn around to communicate with the person behind you, it could give away your presence to an enemy further along your route.

Glow sticks can also make good route or hazard markers and depending on what colours you have available a plan that is thoroughly understood by all group members can be used to confuse hostile followers. For example, while green usually means safe and red indicates danger, you might agree that your group will use them the opposite way. Red shows the path you have taken and green means do not pass.

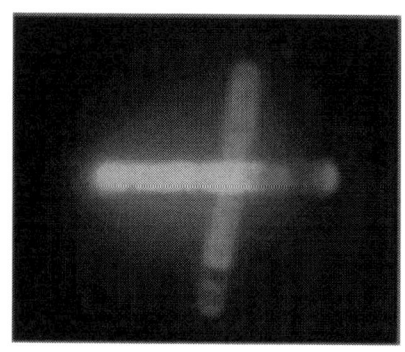

If you only have the one colour then you can use either position or orientation e.g. near the ground means 'don't pass', waist height means 'this way' (make sure it won't fall off!), or a vertical stick for the correct route and a horizontal one for the wrong way.

Make up your own group system and keep it obscure for anyone else. If you are on your own you can use the sticks in a similar way in case you have to backtrack and return to an earlier junction, in which case you might pick up the sticks and use them again further along your new route.

If you are in a flooded area and drop one, it just keeps working. You can often see it even in cloudy water and recover it, though if there is any sort of current it is likely to float away.

An important consideration is that glow sticks are the safest form of illumination in a disaster. They give off no heat nor any electrical current or spark, nor do they need one to initiate them. They are therefore completely safe even if there is any chance of volatile gasses or liquids in the area, or when left unattended even if there are children, animals, or breezes that might upset them and cause them to come into contact with combustible materials. However, do keep them out of reach of children who might try to break them or animals that might chew them!

The sticks will deteriorate over time and most packs will have a 'use by' date. After that date they might no longer work or they might break when bent. The liquid inside is not particularly hazardous but it does stain. As with all life-dated equipment, examine them regularly and replace when required.

Candles

These might be in the form of a tea light, a piece cut from a stearine candle, or a few birthday cake decorations. They are a less attention-grabbing option for light if you don't feel it is safe to have a fire and want to save your torch batteries.

As we examined earlier, they also have important functions in fire lighting and in confined, sheltered spaces can themselves give out useful levels of heat. When used for lamps they are relatively easy to shield both from wind and output in unwanted directions by using a modified tin can, a piece of tree bark, or folded aluminium foil.

First Aid and medicine

If you are in a situation where you need to use a PSK then there has obviously been some sort of major event and there is every chance that you will need to apply first aid to yourself or others.

In an urban environment, where every office and shop and type of public transport will have a first aid kit, you should be able to access something fairly quickly. Nevertheless, there is the chance that you will be trapped somewhere with only your own resources on which to rely, and in a wilderness environment that would certainly be the case.

If you are involved in hazardous activities then it might be appropriate for you to carry an easily portable but fairly comprehensive first aid kit separately in its own container but considered as one part of your PSK. It's your survival at stake; it's your kit. Nobody can say that it all has to be in one tin or pouch; use one container, or a wristband, a belt and a pouch, or whatever works for you, it's your choice!

Otherwise, you can improvise immediate aid and protection for many injuries but might anyway want to pack any or all of the following items:

Adhesive dressings are a standard to help to protect minor injuries from infection and since they are fairly flat they take up little room in your kit. I prefer fabric strips because they can be cut to whatever size is required, are good for blisters as well as cuts, and if good quality seem to stick better than waterproof dressings even when wet. Whatever type you choose, ensure that they have a full covering in order to keep them sterile.

Antiseptic wipe/cream, if available, should be applied after washing the wound but otherwise at least clean the wound as thoroughly as possible. Wipes might be alcohol based, in which case they could also be used as easily ignited tinder, or non-alcohol with an antibacterial ingredient. Either will help.

Pain killers, the stronger the better, can help if you have a serious injury, providing they aren't so strong that they reduce your alertness. You might decide to rely on willpower and stoicism but you are going to have substantial physical and psychological stresses and demands on you so a little relief could be welcome. Be aware that pain relief can tempt you to push the injured area when your body is trying to remind you that it has been damaged and that you might consequently do further harm. To get through the situation you may not have any choice, so do what you need to do but don't go further than that simply from foolish arrogance.

Caffeine tablets are a boost when you are totally shattered but survival demands that you stay alert and push on. However, do remember that when their effect wears off you are going to come down even harder. Some Preppers include a couple of individual sachets of coffee in their kit instead of these tablets and if there is no chance to make a brew they will take the coffee powder straight from the packet into their mouth. The shock to your tongue will wake you up even before the caffeine takes effect but it does work.

Insect repellent is less essential in the UK where bites are less likely to carry nasty diseases but it can be a comfort. Make an assessment of the threat where you work and travel as to whether it deserves a place.

Tweezers might be included as a feature of your pocket knife or you can get a small pair to include in the kit. They are useful for extracting splinters, thorns or stings or, after being sterilised in a flame, for peeling back skin to let you apply antiseptic or to replace it to help cover an open blister.

Antihistamine wipes or creams are sometimes an effective treatment for insect bites or stings or, if you have a known allergy, you might want to carry some pills to reduce the effects. Although they can have a lower level of effectiveness, if you can cope with pills that don't induce tiredness you should choose them.

Super glue is often recommended as a potential wound sealant but if you can cover the wound that is often preferable because it does not also seal in infection. If you do carry glue for this purpose then ensure it is proper medically approved type, not just one intended for household DIY repairs.

Suture sets are the more traditional alternative to glue if you are determined to be macho about it.

Chap Stick will protect not only your lips but also any other area of skin exposed to the cold. You can also use it as a lubricant on an area that is being rubbed, in order to prevent or delay a blister forming, or on a fire drill, zipper, or bolt thread to keep them moving. Smeared onto tinder it will enhance and lengthen the burn time. If you wear spectacles you can rub some on the lenses to prevent them from fogging.

Vaseline can be used for all the same purposes as Chap Stick.

Iodine or Potassium Iodide solution is an effective disinfectant for wounds. It can also be used to sanitise fruits or vegetables potentially contaminated with bacteria or viruses, but it does not work on surfaces that might be contaminated by faeces so good hygiene and thorough cooking is still required.

Potassium Permanganate is also a disinfectant. For wounds use it at a darker shade of solution than when sterilising water. To treat fungal infections on the feet or groin use even darker stained water.

Tampons serve not only their original purpose for women who need them but also open out to provide either a substantial wound covering or a source of cotton wool for use with any of the disinfectants above for cleaning and treating wounds and can plug at least the entry side of a penetrating wound.

Personal meds that you take regularly for any serious condition are an essential feature of your PSK. Consider your situation and how long you believe you might have to rely on your emergency supply before reaching an extended source and use that as a basis for how much you should carry, but do add some extra j.i.c. You should also include a copy of your repeat prescription so that you have proof of need if you do manage to find a source of supply before reaching your own stocks.

Contact lenses or spectacles can easily become lost or broken during a catastrophe so an extra pair is essential if you need them for either general vision or detailed work. I am lucky, I only need reading glasses, but for reading a map or close-in first aid they are still essential. I carry a high magnification pair of very compact folding types wound with bubble wrap to protect them. I usually buy them from either Lidl or pound shops. As a back up, or for even more magnification, I carry a Fresnel lens.

Other

A sewing kit is often included in a PSK but unfortunately the choice is usually a hotel type kit that is fine for a quick repair of clothing under normal circumstances but not robust enough and often larger than necessary for a survival kit.

If you are stuck with a hotel kit, the card could be used for tinder, the needle magnetised as a compass and the buttons as fishing lures (1).

What you need is a couple of stout needles with eyes big enough to take a paracord inner strand or fishing line. Thread them with a double arms length of strong thread, folded and knotted. Push one through a piece of card, wrap the thread around and secure the end under the needle, then do the same with the other. In this way you won't have to fiddle around trying to thread a needle when you are shaking, you will have enough strong yarn for most immediate repairs of outer clothing or equipment, and you will extract one needle and thread without disturbing the other or getting them tangled. Prepping in advance to make things a bit easier when life is hard enough is always a good way to go!

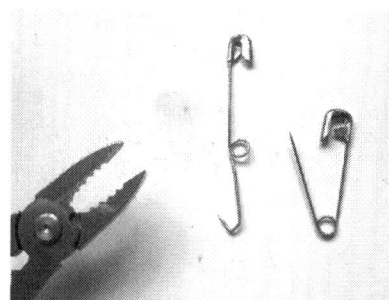

Safety pins can be used as a quick and easy temporary fix before you have chance to use your sewing kit, or they can be adapted to serve as extra fish hooks, or used to lance a blister or dig out a splinter or sting, or secure a bandage or sling, fasten together the edges of a blanket to make a sleeping bag, or around a stick in a shelter sheet as an attachment point, or as a replacement zipper pull, or a hook or spike in a trap for small animals or birds, or ... whatever else your imagination will stretch to. Suffice to say, for something that takes up so little space and adds so little weight, it is well worth including a few.

Foil blankets and Suspender clips can be an excellent, lightweight accessory. The blankets will take up too much room in a survival tin but are an option for pouches or other forms of carry and do provide immediate, if sometimes flimsy shelter. The clips are small enough to be included in any kit and offer a secure, easy-to-use way of fixing cordage to thin materials like the blankets, refuse sacks, or hay bale covers. As an alternative you can use a stone, twig, nut or rolled up vegetation to wrap in the shelter material and then tie cordage around it but the clips are less likely to cause damage and will extend the useful life of the thin stuff. For any male Prepper that might be embarrassed about buying them, they are available from survival equipment outlets that won't make assumptions about any nefarious motives.

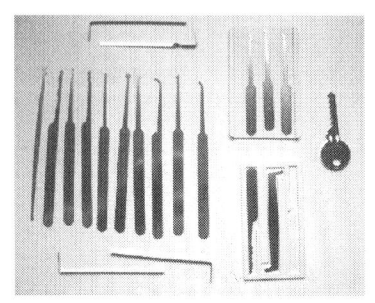

Bump keys and lock picks are not tools for the beginning Prepper and are definitely one for the urban kit. There are potential legal challenges that you have to consider when carrying these but for those who learn to use them efficiently they offer covert access to shelter, supplies, or escape routes where otherwise you would be reduced to smashing or hack-sawing your way through. They are available perfectly legally from suppliers to locksmiths and hobbyists and some come with clear and helpful usage guides. Otherwise there are plenty of books available on the subject. Some pick and key suppliers also sell transparent or cut-away locks that are great help in learning to use the tools.

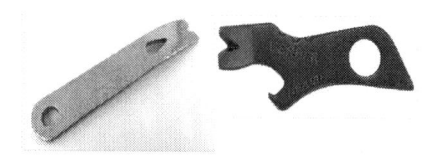

Mini pry bars are a potentially useful addition or alternative to the lock picks. Some (though not all – test what you buy!) are surprisingly robust. Some are simply a pry bar; others offer a range of features. All the ones we would consider for a PSK are sized to be carried on a key ring, so you aren't going to be opening warehouse doors with them but for getting into lockers, cupboards and the like they have their uses.

A Chain and padlock can be used to smash glass to gain entry to supplies, a vehicle or locked premises or to secure an access behind you when you have found somewhere to hide or rest or if you fear you are being pursued. If challenged, say it was for your bicycle but somebody stole everything but the wheel it was fixed to.

Alternatively it will extend your reach and impact if you need it to defend yourself. In the latter case, don't let your enemy see your weapon before you swing. When you do, don't hold back but don't swing through either; strike your target hard and then snatch the chain back to prepare for another strike and prevent them from grabbing the weapon.

If the hostile does not go down immediately then quickly hit again at a different target, and again and again if necessary, until they are either down and you can run off or they do.

The head, face (eyes, nose or jaws if it is a predatory animal), shoulder, elbows, wrists, knees and ankles are your most effective targets. If you are surprised and they are too close for you to swing and you cannot back off to give you space, then punch with the chain wrapped around your fist or hit with the padlock grasped in your hand.

Adhesive tape such an electrical, duct or 'gorilla' tape has gained a place in many kits. It can be used as cordage, a wound dressing, a temporary clothing repair or many other things. Some types will burn and can be used as tinder but electrical tape and others is deliberately made to be flame resistant so do check if you expect to use it in that role. Brightly coloured forms can be used for signalling.

Cash and coins can often be useful in an urban environment. Small denomination notes can be used in some machines or to buy your way onto transport, especially after you have escaped from a highly affected area to somewhere facilities are still operating. Coins can get you out of a car park, or source supplies, street maps or tickets from vending machines. In wilder areas they can be used as catapult ammo or as sinkers for fishing.

If you are travelling overseas then a supply of both local currency and well regarded foreign money is often acceptable. Depending where you are, that might be US dollars, Roubles, Euros, or Yuan Renminbi. The British pound will find fewer takers but gold sovereigns have been a standard for military and security survival kits for centuries, and other gold – or to a lesser extent silver – coins or jewellery can be used for barter. Some countries now seem to be developing strange laws regarding the movement of gold coins through their borders, so do check before travelling, or hide your stash well.

Survival references can be a real bonus when stress and fatigue impose challenges on your memory. A small sheet or set of cards holding information on plant identification, trap triggers, emergency signals, and other essential topics will help you to avoid potentially serious mistakes or remind you of easier ways to do things. In foreign countries you could include a selection of local words or phrases applicable to emergency situations or pictures to which you can point if you don't know the relevant word.

Whichever you choose, ensure it is on waterproof paper or card.

You could get a lot more info on a data card or usb drive but access could be an issue (1).

These are the possibly less vital but still extremely useful items that you might include in your PSK if you have the room and weight allowance.

Basic kit lists

Wilderness and Military

- Cutting tool
- Cordage
- Saw
- Lighter, matches, ferro rod & striker, Fresnel lens
- Tinder
- Candle
- Condom or poly bag
- Purification tablets
- Aluminium baking foil
- Tin opener
- Brass or steel wire
- Arrow heads
- Fishing kit – hooks, line, sinkers, fake flies & maggots
- Duct tape
- Rubber bands
- Button or other small compass
- Paper and pencil with eraser
- Torch & spare batteries
- Mini glow sticks
- Whistle
- Medical items – adhesive dressing, antiseptic wipe, pain killers, personal meds, contact lenses or glasses
- Needles & thread
- Safety pins
- Sharpening stone
- Survival instructions

Urban

- Cash and coins
- Cordage
- Knife or other blade
- Lighter, matches, ferro rod & striker, Fresnel lens
- Tinder
- Water purification tablets
- Tin opener
- Brass or steel wire
- Electrical tape
- Rubber bands
- Hacksaw blade
- Mini pry bar
- Lock picks and bump key
- Chain and padlock
- Button or other small compass
- Paper and pencil with eraser
- Marker pen
- Torch
- Mini glow sticks
- Whistle
- Medical items – adhesive dressing, antiseptic wipe, pain killers, personal meds, contact lenses or glasses, prescription
- Needles & thread
- Safety pins
- Mini USB drive or data card
- Personal photo

Summary

This is a book intended to provide information that will be of help to people who find themselves in emergency situations away from their home and without their usual resources, due to the effects of a disaster.

Those who sensibly prepare for such situations will ensure that they have some equipment to help them deal with the challenges they would face. Hopefully the information and advice offered in these chapters will have helped you to choose some of those items that will best suit you, the events you believe might occur, and the ways you will choose to deal with them.

I have done my best to make it primarily, though not solely, applicable to UK citizens, because most of the other books on the market are written for other areas.

It is aimed at skills and resources available to most inhabitants of these islands, but includes some information especially useful abroad.

If the preceding pages help to prepare you for what might be to come, then that is the purpose of the book and I hope that it will be of use to you when you most need it, but that you never do!

Acknowledgements

I would like to thank the people who so generously offered their assistance during the writing of this book, especially Liz (RT), who gave invaluable feedback and advice. Her contributions are noted throughout with (1). A big Thank you; your participation helped this become a work I can hope all readers will enjoy.

In addition, my thanks go to my wife Patricia, for putting up with my early mornings and late nights with my eyes and mind focussed only on my computer screen while walls went unpainted and fittings unfixed.

Recommended suppliers

The Friendly Swede via Amazon.co.uk
http://www.edcgear.co.uk
http://www.heinnie.com/
https://www.polymathproducts.co.uk/shop
http://www.withoutakey.co.uk/

About the author

Son of a Scottish mother and Yorkshire father, David Eric Crossley was raised in Yorkshire. After a number of unsatisfying jobs, he joined the forces in 1970 and was a soldier for over 20 years.

Qualified as an instructor in Nuclear Biological and Chemical Warfare, Combat Survival, Urban and Counter-revolutionary Warfare, Signals, Advanced First Aid, Light Rescue and Fire fighting, among other things, he served in Africa, Asia, the Gulf, Central and South America and Europe. He has lived through the reality and aftermath of wars and counter-terrorist operations, and as an advisor and rescuer during Aid to the Civil Powers missions after major disasters overseas.

After leaving the forces, David settled in Scotland. He worked as Training Manager Scotland for the British Red Cross for 4 years including training overseas service and emergency response volunteers, and now works as an independent survival consultant and writer.

David has been writing professionally since the 1980s and has had over 100 magazine articles and short stories published in outdoors, survival, military, business and general interest media. He has also published Bugging In and Bugging Out which are detailed books on those subjects, and There Falls No Shadow - the first novel of a post-apocalyptic series - and compiled, edited and wrote much of an urban survival reference, published as Streetcraft, for Ludlow Survivors Group.

Check out David's other books at: http://www.tfns.co.uk or on Amazon.UK

David welcomes feedback from readers of his work. Please email him at: books@decrossley.co.uk

Printed in Great Britain
by Amazon